The Lab Manual
to accompany

Henry

THE EFFECTIVE READER
Fourth Edition

Mary Dubbé
Thomas Nelson Community College

PEARSON

Boston   Columbus   Indianapolis   New York   San Francisco   Upper Saddle River

Amsterdam   Cape Town   Dubai   London   Madrid   Milan   Munich   Paris   Montreal   Toronto

Delhi   Mexico City   São Paulo   Sydney   Hong Kong   Seoul   Singapore   Taipei   Tokyo

The Lab Manual to accompany Henry, *The Effective Reader, Fourth Edition*

Copyright © 2015, 2011, and 2008, Pearson Education, Inc.

PEARSON

www.pearsonhighered.com

ISBN 10: 0-321-98854-X

ISBN 13: 978-0-321-98854-6

CONTENTS

For Students:

This Lab Manual is a collection of 78 activities designed to provide additional practice and enrichment for the skills in *The Effective Reader*. Each chapter consists of six lab activities that will provide you with additional practice and assessment of your skills.

You will practice applying the strategies you are learning to numerous textbook paragraphs and longer passages from a wide range of academic disciplines. You will continue to learn new vocabulary in many activities, practice identifying main ideas and supporting details, use outlines and concept maps to make sure you understand the reading selections, and practice your inference skills in the contexts of excerpts taken primarily from current college textbooks.

This lab manual also includes a skills awareness inventory sheet for each of the tutorial tests that you may take before you begin the course as well as achievement tests to discover how much you have learned by the end of the course. Three pairs of tests are available: one is specifically designed for students in Florida who must pass the Florida State Basic Skills Exit Test, a second is for Texas students who need to take the THEA, and a third is intended for more general use. (Your instructor will provide the most appropriate one for you.) Answer sheets are available in the back of the Lab Manual as well as report forms that foster metacognition. These report forms can be used as a portfolio activity to help you assess your learning and growth.

Finally, at the end of the manual is a report form where you can record your grades and keep track of your progress. Mastering these skills will ensure that you are effectively prepared for your academic subjects.

For Instructors:

The Lab Manual is a collection of 78 activities designed to provide additional practice and enrichment for the skills in *The Effective Reader*. Each chapter consists of six lab activities that can be used to add flexibility and interest to the classroom or for additional practice and for assessment purposes.

These lab activities provide students with a range of opportunities to practice becoming effective readers. The chapters of *The Effective Reader* include numerous practices, applications, review tests, and mastery tests. The Lab Manual offers two practice exercises, two review tests and two mastery tests that mirror the design of the text and emphasize the reading skills and applications students need to succeed in college. Students apply the strategies they are learning to numerous textbook paragraphs and longer passages from a wide range of academic disciplines.

Each activity in the Lab Manual is carefully constructed to ensure that students understand the purpose of the activity and can complete it successfully. The practice exercises begin with a succinct statement of the objective. The Answer Key to the Lab Manual can be found online at www.pearsonhighered.com/henry and by choosing *The Effective Reader*. A report form is available at the end of the manual for students to keep a record of their scores and to track their progress.

The lab manual also includes a skills awareness inventory sheet for each of the tutorial tests that students may take before they begin the course as well as achievement tests to discover how much they have learned by the end of the course. Three pairs of tests are available for students using *The Effective Reader*: one is specifically designed for students in Florida who must pass the Florida State Basic Skills Exit Test, a second is for Texas students who need to take the THEA, and a third is intended for more general use. The answer sheets are available in the back of the Lab Manual as well as report forms that foster metacognition. These report forms can be used as a portfolio activity to help assess student learning and growth. The tutorial tests appear in the Instructor's Manual that accompanies *The Effective Reader*, or you can access the tutorial tests by going to http://www.pearsonhighered.com/henry and selecting *The Effective Reader*.

ABOUT THE SERIES

The Skilled Reader, 4e (available in 2014)
The Effective Reader, 4e (available in 2014)
The Master Reader, 4e (available in 2014)

The series of skills-based textbooks, written by D. J. Henry of Daytona Beach Community College, features plentiful opportunities for students to practice individual and combined reading skills on high-interest passages from both textbooks and popular sources. Basic reading comprehension and vocabulary skills are addressed, and critical reading skills are introduced in careful step-by-step fashion.

The Henry series focuses students' attention on how their skills apply to reading college textbooks. The books also emphasize the importance of visuals, in addition to text, as valuable sources of information. Students are asked to respond to visuals throughout the series in Visual Vocabulary features. The Lab Manual offers 78 activities designed to provide additional practice and enrichment for all the topics in each book.

Mary Dubbé, teaches developmental integrated reading and writing classes at Thomas Nelson Community College. She graduated from West Virginia University with an M.S. degree in language arts and an M.A. in reading. She has over 25 years of experience in preparing college students to be effective readers and successful students. In addition to teaching, Mary is the director of learning communities on her campus, has presented workshops at several state and national conferences, and is currently the president of the Virginia Association of Developmental Education.

Name_____ Section _____ Date _____ Score (number correct) _____ x 10 = _____

Objective: To use the SQ3R reading system to read and answer questions about the following selection from a college speech textbook.

A. Directions: Read the passage and answer the questions that follow.

Initiating Conversations

Speakers and listeners have to work together to make conversation an effective and satisfying experience. **Conversational management** includes initiating, maintaining, and closing conversations. Several approaches to initiating or opening a conversation exist. *Self-references* say something about yourself. Such references may be of the "name, rank and serial number" type—for example: "My name is Joe. I'm from Omaha." On the first day of class, students might say, "I'm worried about this class" or "I took this instructor last semester; she was excellent."

Other-references say something about the other person or ask a question: "I like that sweater." "Didn't we meet at Charlie's?" Of course, there are pitfalls here. Generally, it is best not to comment on the person's race ("My uncle married a Korean") or physical disability ("It must be awful to be confined to a wheelchair"). *Relational references* say something about the two of you: for example, "May I buy you a drink?" "Would you like to dance?" or simply, "May I join you?" *Context references* say something about the physical, social, cultural, or temporal context. The familiar, "Do you have the time?" is a reference of this type. But you can be more creative and say, for example, "This restaurant seems very friendly," or "This Dalí is fantastic."

> —Adapted from De Vito, *The Interpersonal Communication Book,* 10th ed., p. 218.

_____1. While surveying this article, the effective reader would first notice _____.
   a.   the questions in the 2nd paragraph
   b.   the examples of approaches to initiate conversation
   c.   the word *references* within both paragraphs
   d.   the phrases in bold print and in italics

_____2. Which of the following would be helpful to know prior to reading this article?
   a.   background about Korea
   b.   an explanation of the word *references*
   c.   background about Charlie's
   d.   information about common disabilities

_____3. Which of the following questions will help the effective reader focus on the main ideas of this article?
   a.   What is a Dalí?
   b.   What are some tips to overcome shyness?
   c.   How can conversation be managed?
   d.   Where are the best places to meet interesting people?

1

_____4. According to the information in the first paragraph, *self-references* _____.
     a. ask questions about the listener
     b. ask questions about the location
     c. are comments about the person in charge
     d. are personal comments about oneself

_____5. The phrase *other-references* in the second paragraph most likely means _____.
     a. research material
     b. former employers who can vouch for one's work history
     c. literary works
     d. statements or questions that refer to the listener

_____6. An example of a *context reference* is _____.
     a. "The lead singer of this band is from Haiti."
     b. "Have you heard this band before today?"
     c. "I like your taste in music."
     d. "This is the tenth time I have listened to this group perform."

_____7. Which of the following questions concerning this passage would most likely appear on a test?
     a. Explain the term conversational management.
     b. Define the term *self-reference* and give an example.
     c. What is the difference between a *relational reference* and an *other-reference*?
     d. All of the above

B. Directions: Read this passage and answer the following questions.

The nation's large publishing houses (those with 100 or more employees) publish 80 percent of the books sold each year, but some of the nation's publishers are small operations with fewer than ten employees. These publishers are called *small presses*, and they counterbalance the corporate world of large advances and multi-media subsidiary rights. Small presses do not have the budgets of the large houses, but their size means they can specialize in specific topics, such as the environment or bicycling, or in specific types of writing that are unattractive to large publishers, such as poetry.

        —Adapted from Biagi, *Media Impact: An Introduction to Mass Media*, 8th ed., p. 40.

_____8. Which of the following questions most effectively reflects the main idea of this passage?
     a. Where did small publishing houses originate?
     b. How do smaller publishing companies compete with large publishing houses?
     c. What are the characteristics of small presses?
     d. Why are some types of writing unattractive to large publishers?

_____9. According to the context, *small presses* are _____.
     a. companies that publish unimportant material
     b. publishing companies with fewer than employees
     c. small publishing companies that publish material of poor quality
     d. miniature printing presses used in the publication of short documents

_____10. What is one advantage that small presses have over large publishing houses?
   a.   They have larger budgets.
   b.   They publish 20 percent more books than large companies.
   c.   They can specialize in specific topics or specific types of writing.
   d.   They have more employees to do the work.

Name_____ Section _____ Date _____ Score (number correct) _____ x 10 = _____

Objective: To use the SQ3R reading system to read a selection from a college psychology textbook.

Directions: Read the following excerpt and answer the questions that follow.

Primacy and Recency Effects

1 In a typical memory experiment, a participant may be asked to study a list of words and recall as many of the items as possible so that the researcher can determine whether the information was transferred from short-term memory storage to long-term memory. If the list is 30 or 40 items long, such experiments typically show an overall recall rate of 20%, but memory is not even throughout the list. Recall is higher for words at the beginning of a series than for those in the middle, a phenomenon termed the **primacy effect**. This effect occurs because no information related to the task at hand is already stored in short-term storage; at the moment a person begins a new task, attention to new stimuli is at its peak. In addition, words at the beginning of a series get to be rehearsed more often, allowing them to be transferred to long-term memory. Thus, the primacy effect is associated with long-term memory processes.

2 However, recall is even higher for words at the end of the series—a phenomenon termed the **recency effect**. These more recently presented items are still being held in short-term storage, where they can be actively rehearsed without interference as they are encoded for long-term memory. The recency effect is thus thought to be related to short-term storage.

3 When one item on a list differs from the others—for example, an adjective in a series of common nouns or a longer word in a series of short ones—the one different item is learned more easily. This is the phenomenon called the **von Restorff effect**.

—Adapted from Lefton & Brannon, *Psychology*, 8th ed., pp. 283–285.

_____1. When skimming the title and first paragraph, an effective reader would ask all of the following *except* _____.
    a. What does the word *primacy* mean?
    b. What does the word *recency* mean?
    c. What do I already know about sociology?
    d. What do I already know about short-term memory?

_____2. A question the reader would formulate while skimming the passage would include all of the following *except* _____.
    a. What is the primacy effect?
    b. What is the recency effect?
    c. What is the von Restorff effect?
    d. Who conducts research on memory?

_____3. Which line would an active learner probably highlight as a main idea?
      a. In a typical memory experiment, a participant may be asked to study a list of words and recall as many of the items as possible so that the researcher can determine whether the information transferred from short-term storage to long-term memory.
      b. If the list is 30 to 40 items long, such experiments typically show an overall recall rate of 20%, but memory is not even throughout the list.
      c. Recall is higher for words at the beginning of a series than for those in the middle, a phenomenon termed the **primacy effect**.
      d. The primacy effect is associated with long-term memory.

_____4. In paragraph 2, the word _phenomenon_ probably means _____.
      a. sight
      b. organization
      c. experience
      d. noun

_____5. Which of the following would an effective reader highlight in this passage?
      a. the entire first paragraph
      b. the examples provided in paragraph 3
      c. the bold-faced words and their definitions
      d. all of the last paragraph

_____6. Questions an active learner might pose as he or she skims the material would include all of the following _except_ _____.
      a. How can the von Restorff effect help in my own study routine?
      b. Would studying in smaller chunks of time with short breaks in between help me to improve my memory?
      c. What should I do on my study breaks?
      d. How can perceptual imagery help me in my studies?

_____7. According to the context, the best definition of _recall_ is _____.
      a. a request to return something
      b. dismiss from office
      c. resemble something
      d. remember something

_____8. From this article, the effective reader could assume that _____.
      a. the beginning of a list is the most difficult part to recall
      b. the middle of a list is the most difficult part to recall
      c. the end of a list is the most difficult part to recall
      d. placement in a list has no effect on ability to recall

_____9. The _von Restorff effect_ concludes that _____.
      a. a differing item in a series is easier to remember
      b. similar items in a series are easier to remember
      c. items in a series are nearly impossible to remember
      d. things that are similar are easier to remember than things that are different

_____10. Which sentence best summarizes this article?

    a. Experiments show that the recall average of a list is 20%.

    b. The primacy effect is a phenomenon that emerges in memory research.

    c. Experiments show that many variables can affect one's ability to recall items in a list.

    d. Memory is often a subject explored by researchers.

Name_____ Section _____ Date _____ Score (number correct) _____ x 10 = _____

Directions: Use effective reading skills to answer the questions that follow this passage.

Students Sing the Blues

Campus Blues

1 The stressors of college life, such as anxiety over relationships, pressure to get good grades and win social acceptance, abuse of alcohol and other drugs, poor diet, and lack of sleep can create a toxic cocktail. It is no surprise that depression on college campuses is a huge problem. According to a longitudinal study of students who sought help at campus over a 13-year period, sources of depression changed from relationship and money problems in the 1980s to more serious forms of stress-related anxiety in later years, paralleling trends in society as a whole.

2 International students are particularly vulnerable to mental health concerns. Being far from home without the security of family and friends can exacerbate problems and make coping difficult. Most campuses have cultural centers and other services available; however, many students do not utilize them.

Treating Depression

3 The best treatment involves determining the person's type and degree of depression and its possible causes. Both psychotherapeutic and pharmacological modes of treatment are recommended for clinical (severe and prolonged) depression. Drugs often relieve the symptoms of depression, such as loss of sleep or appetite, while psychotherapy can be equally helpful for improving the ability to function. In some cases, psychotherapy alone may be the most successful treatment. The most common psychotherapeutic treatments for depression are **cognitive therapy** and **interpersonal therapy.**

—Donatelle, *Access to Health*, 10th ed., p. 59.

_____1. While surveying this article, what should an effective reader first notice?
    a.   the words *psychotherapeutic* and *pharmacological*
    b.   the references to numbers: *13-year period* and *1980s*
    c.   the bold-faced heading **Treating Depression** and the bold-faced words in the last paragraph
    d.   the name of the author

_____2. An effective reader might first think this article focuses on the music genre, the blues. What adjustment will the reader make after completing the survey?
    a.   The reader will realize this is the correct topic.
    b.   The reader will realize this article is about depression among college students and recommended ways to treat it.
    c.   The reader will understand that this article is a humorous description of campus life.
    d.   The reader will realize that the focus of this article is on the definition of therapy.

_____3. All of the following questions will help the effective reader focus on the main ideas of this article *except* _____.
   a. What causes stress among college students?
   b. How is depression treated?
   c. Which college major causes the highest levels of stress in students?
   d. What do cognitive therapy and interpersonal therapy mean?

_____4. This article suggests that _____.
   a. All students are equally at risk for depression.
   b. International students are more at risk for mental-health concerns than American students.
   c. College life has become much less stressful over the years.
   d. Lack of sleep is the most common reason for stress in college students.

_____5. Upon examining the way *toxic* is used in paragraph 1, which educated guess should the effective reader make about the meaning of a *toxic cocktail*?
   a. a dangerous alcoholic drink
   b. a harmful combination of things that cause stress
   c. a poisonous substance
   d. a contaminating pollutant

_____6. What is the most likely definition of *vulnerable* in paragraph 2?
   a. resistant
   b. fortified
   c. at risk
   d. closed

_____7. The word *exacerbate* in paragraph 2 most likely means _____.
   a. improve   b. move out   c. inform   d. worsen

_____8. What logical conclusion can the effective reader make about a clinical depression from this article? A clinical depression is _____.
   a. an unemotional illness
   b. a low-pressure area
   c. an experimental design
   d. a long-term and serious psychological disorder

_____9. A pharmacological mode of treating depression would most likely involve the use of
   a. prescription drugs.
   b. journal writing.
   c. talking with a counselor.
   d. upbeat music.

_____10. Which sentence best summarizes the main ideas of this selection?
   a. Depression among college students is increasing, but there are effective treatments for this mental health disorder.
   b. Psychotherapy is an effective way to treat depression among college students.
   c. Depression is a serious mental health disorder.
   d. International students are particularly vulnerable to depression.

Name_____ Section _____ Date _____ Score (number correct) _____ x 10 = _____

Directions: Use effective reading skills to answer the questions that follow this passage.

Fighting Poverty, Fighting to Learn

1 What can a single person do to address the harsh realities of inequality? One answer that sociologists often give to this question is: "Try teaching, at least for a while, and teach somewhere where people are desperate for dedicated teachers."

2 In the face of extreme poverty and injustice, and against the systematic exploitation of those who have little by the few who seem to have everything, what can a teacher accomplish? We can never fully answer this question, but there are teaching situations around the world and in our own country where it will be obvious that teaching the basics of reading and writing is a primary route to social change. Consider, for example, the research of sociologist John L. Hammond among the peasants of El Salvador, where literacy instruction was a key element in the struggle for equality and democracy.

3 Hammond's focus was on the "**popular teachers**" who challenged the rote-learning of traditional classrooms and who worked among the peasants teaching basic literacy. They threw themselves with great energy into their work among the children and adult peasants who came to them after their work in the fields. By teaching illiterate children to read and write, they were giving them the tools needed to begin to understand the social conditions that made them poor and prevented them from taking a full part in building the democratic institutions of their societies.

4 Popular education in Central America was often critical of the status quo, and therefore at times it became the target of oppression by those in power. But teaching literacy, whether to rural children and adults in Central America, women in the Islamic world, or people in poor communities in our own society, always entails some controversy and risk. That is what makes it such a valuable endeavor and such a unique learning experience for students and teachers as well.

—Adapted from Kornblum, *Sociology in a Changing World*, 9th ed., p. 254.

_____1. While surveying this article, the effective reader would first notice _____.
   a. the reasons why people become teachers
   b. the absence of research studies
   c. the types of students in the last paragraph
   d. the heading and the phrase **popular teachers**

_____2. Which of the following would be helpful to know prior to reading this article?
   a. the kind of training required to teach literacy skills to those who are disadvantaged
   b. effective ways of eliminating poverty around the world
   c. background information about the struggle for equality and democracy in El Salvador
   d. research studies about the effectiveness of disregarding traditional classroom methods

11

_____3. Which of the following questions will help the effective reader focus upon the main ideas of this selection?
   a. How can learning be a tool for fighting poverty?
   b. What are the requirements to become a teacher?
   c. Where can information be found about the struggle for equality in El Salvador?
   d. What are the advantages and disadvantages of teaching?

_____4. According to the information in this passage, which of the following statements is true?
   a. Teachers who are not popular will probably accomplish very little.
   b. Traditional classrooms are ineffective in areas of poverty.
   c. Educating peasants is sometimes viewed as a threat to the wealthy upper classes.
   d. The peasants of El Salvador were never able to achieve equality or democracy.

_____5. According to information in paragraph three, "**popular teachers**" _____.
   a. usually teach in the best schools
   b. often disregard traditional teaching methods
   c. are well-liked because they often don't enforce rules
   d. are often exploited

_____6. Which information will help the effective reader better understand the ideas in paragraph four?
   a. Background information about women in the Islamic world
   b. background information about providing unique learning experiences
   c. background information about the risks and controversy of teaching literacy in Central America
   d. background information about politics in poor countries

_____7. From this article, the effective reader could assume that _____.
   a. teaching literacy skills to the poor can change a country
   b. the people of Central America resent education in their country
   c. education in many Central American countries is reserved for men only
   d. teachers can accomplish very little in the face of extreme poverty and injustice

B. Directions: Read this passage and answer the following questions.

Parenting Styles

1 *Authoritarian parenting combines high control with little warmth.* These parents lay down the rules and expect them to be followed without discussion. Hard work, respect, and obedience are what authoritarian parents wish to cultivate in their children. There is little give-and-take between parent and child because authoritarian parents do not consider children's needs or wishes.

2 *Authoritative parenting combines a fair degree of parental control with being warm and responsive to children.* Authoritative parents explain rules and encourage discussion. An authoritative parent might explain why children can't do something and encourage them to discuss the issues involved.

3 *Permissive parenting offers warmth and caring but little parental control.* These parents generally accept their children's behavior and punish them infrequently. An indulgent-permissive parent would readily agree to a child's requests, simply because it is something the child wants to do.

   —Adapted from Kail and Cavanaugh, *Human Development: A Life-Span View*, 4th ed., p. 268.

_____8. Which of the following questions most effectively reflects the main idea of this passage?
    a. Why do people offer differ in their parenting styles?
    b. How do parents create happy and healthy children?
    c. What are the different styles of parenting?
    d. What is the most common parenting style?

_____9. What information is important to note during a preview of this article?
    a. the example of authoritative parenting
    b. the term *indulgent-permissive* in the third paragraph
    c. the example of an indulgent-permissive parent
    d. the words and definitions in bold face print and italics

_____10. While reading and studying this article, an effective reader should _____.
    a. note and learn the difference between authoritarian and authoritative parenting
    b. highlight all of the sentences in the first paragraph
    c. question the accuracy of this information
    d. disregard the sentences that are not in italics and bold face print

Name_____ Section _____ Date _____ Score (number correct) _____ x 10 = _____

Directions: Read the passage and answer the questions that follow.

1 Having lampooned the Eisenhower administration as <u>stodgy</u> and unimaginative, President Kennedy made a show of his style and wit. He <u>flouted</u> convention by naming his younger brother Robert attorney general. "I can't see that it's wrong to give him a little legal experience before he goes out to practice law," the president quipped. Kennedy also prided himself on being a man of letters, winner of the Pulitzer Prize for *Profiles in Courage.* He quoted Robert Frost and Dante. He played and replayed recordings of Winston Churchill, hoping to imprint the great orator's sonorous cadences on his own flat Bostonian vowels. At the instigation of his elegant wife, Jacqueline, Kennedy surrounded himself with the finest intellects at glittering White House <u>galas</u> to honor Nobel Prize winners and celebrated artists.

2 Kennedy's youthful senior staff boasted impressive scholarly credentials. His national security advisor, McGeorge Bundy, had been dean of the faculty at Harvard (and the first undergraduate at Yale to receive perfect scores in three college entrance examinations). Secretary of Defense Robert McNamara also had taught at Harvard before becoming the first non-family member to head the Ford Motor Company. The administration constituted, as journalist David Halberstam observed later, somewhat ruefully, "the best and the brightest."

3 Kennedy's campaign slogan—"Let's get this country moving again"—was embodied in his own active life. He played rugged games of touch football with the press corps and romped with his young children in the Oval Office. In an article for *Sports Illustrated* entitled "The Soft American" and published just after the election, Kennedy complained that television, movies, and a comfortable lifestyle had made too many young people flabby. His earliest presidential initiative was a physical fitness campaign in the schools.

4 Kennedy's image of youthful vigor ("vigah," as he pronounced the word) was enhanced by the beauty and presence of Jacqueline, whose wide-eyed diffidence was commonly misunderstood and universally admired as regal bearing. The image was enhanced by Lerner and Loew's musical *Camelot*, which opened a few weeks before the inauguration. Its evocation of King Arthur, who sought to lead his virile young knights in challenges of great and good, suggested the Kennedy White House. (The musical became a favorite of the president; he often listened to the cast recordings before going to sleep.) All Washington seemed aglow with excitement and energy. In the words of the administration's chief chronicler, Arthur M. Schlesinger Jr. (another former Harvard professor): "Never had girls seemed so pretty, tunes so melodious, and evenings so blithe and unconstrained."

5 Never, too, had the substance of an administration been so closely identified with the style of its president. But the dazzle was misleading. Although quick-witted and intelligent, Kennedy was no intellectual. His favorite reading was the James Bond spy novels of Ian Fleming. He never admitted it publicly, but most of *Profiles of Courage* had been ghostwritten by paid writers.

6 Nor did the president embody physical fitness. Congenital back problems, aggravated by war injuries, forced Kennedy to use crutches or a cane in private and to take heavy doses of painkillers and amphetamines. The president's permanent "tan" did not result from outdoor exercise, as the public assumed, but from Addison's disease, an often fatal failure of the adrenal glands for which Kennedy gave himself daily injections of cortisone. Though he publicly denied it, Kennedy was chronically ill throughout his presidency.

—Adapted from Carnes & Garraty, *The American Nation,* 11th ed., pp. 789–90.

_____1. Which question would an effective reader ask while reading this passage?
- a. Who was the president of France during Kennedy's administration?
- b. Which of President Kennedy's brothers is currently a U.S. senator?
- c. What do I already know about President Kennedy?
- d. Where was Kennedy born?

_____2. Which question would be helpful for an effective reader to consider while reading this passage?
- a. What do I know about the play *Camelot* and the outcome of King Arthur?
- b. How many members of Kennedy's staff attended Harvard University?
- c. What other magazines did Kennedy read besides *Sports Illustrated*?
- d. What were Kennedy's favorite TV shows?

_____3. According to the context of paragraph 1, the best definition of *stodgy* is _____.
- a. cheerful
- b. creative
- c. dull and boring
- d. inspiring enthusiasm

_____4. According to the context of paragraph 1, the best definition of *flouted* is _____.
- a. mocked
- b. obeyed
- c. created
- d. followed

_____5. According to the context of paragraph 1, the best definition of *galas* is _____.
- a. public tours
- b. work sessions
- c. festive occasions
- d. camping trips

_____6. Which mental picture would an effective reader create while reading paragraph 3?
- a. Kennedy playing touch football
- b. Kennedy watching TV and eating pork rinds
- c. Kennedy watching movies and eating popcorn
- d. Kennedy napping in the Oval Office

_____7. Which mental picture would an effective reader create while reading paragraph 6?
- a. Kennedy in a hospital bed
- b. Knights in armor and beautiful women
- c. Studious scholars in dimly lit libraries
- d. Long lines at the gas pumps

_____8.   Which is the best restatement of paragraph 2?
      a.   Kennedy's staff was comprised of some of the country's most intellectually elite, who had proved their success in other venues.
      b.   Most of Kennedy's staff members were too young to serve in the difficult positions in which they had been appointed.
      c.   While he was very bright, Secretary of Defense Robert McNamara should have stayed at the Ford Motor Company.
      d.   Though very bright, many of Kennedy's staff members did not have enough government experience to serve the country's best interests.

_____9.   Which is the best restatement of paragraph 3?
      a.   Kennedy was responsible for the establishment of MTV.
      b.   Kennedy was a strong critic of the film industry.
      c.   Kennedy was concerned that the country's students were spending too much time in front of the television and not enough time in our nation's libraries.
      d.   Kennedy was concerned that young people were becoming less active, so one of his first accomplishments was his school physical fitness campaign.

_____10. What is the best restatement of paragraphs 5–6?
      a.   Kennedy was largely responsible for the popularity of the James Bond films.
      b.   Much of what the public saw in President Kennedy was based on the image he presented rather than the reality that existed.
      c.   The president was not as physically fit as he was portrayed by the press.
      d.   Though a well-kept secret, a chronic illness plagued the president.

Name_____ Section _____ Date _____ Score (number correct) _____ x 10 = _____

Directions: Read the complete sociology section and answer the questions that follow.

Marriage and Family in Global Perspective

1 To better understand U.S. patterns of marriage and family, let's first look at how customs differ around the world. This will give us a context for interpreting our own experiences in this vital social institution.

What Is a Family?

2 "What is a family, anyway?" asked William Sayres (1992) at the beginning of an article on this topic. By this question, he meant that although the family is so significant to humanity that it is universal— every human group in the world organizes its members in families—the world's cultures display so much variety that the term *family* is difficult to define. For example, although the Western world regards a family as a husband, wife, and children, other groups have family forms in which men have more than one wife (**polygyny**) or women more than one husband (**polyandry**). How about the obvious? Can we define family as the approved group into which children are born? This would overlook the Banaro of New Guinea. In this group, a young woman must give birth before she can marry—and she *cannot* marry the father of her child (Murdock 1949).

3 And so it goes. For just about every element you might regard as essential to marriage or family, some group has a different custom. Consider the sex of the bride and groom. Although in almost every instance the bride and groom are female and male, there are exceptions. In some Native American tribes, a man or woman who wanted to be a member of the opposite sex went through a ceremony (*berdache*) and was declared a member of the opposite sex. Not only did the "new" man or woman do the tasks associated with his or her new sex, but also the individual was allowed to marry. In this instance, the husband and wife were of the same biological sex. In the contemporary world, Denmark (in 1989), Norway (in 1993), Sweden (in 1995), and Holland (in 1998) have legalized same-sex marriages.

—Henslin, *Essentials of Sociology*, 5th ed., pp. 324–326.

_____1. After surveying the title, headings, and first paragraph, which would an effective reader anticipate to follow?
   a. reasons people choose to marry
   b. the history of marriage and how it has changed over time
   c. the definition of marriage and family and the role culture plays in each
   d. a comparison of American families past and present

_____2. Questions a student might form after surveying and before reading this passage would include all of the following *except*
   a. What is family?
   b. What kind of person would make a good spouse?
   c. How might a global perspective of family differ from what I already know?
   d. Are families the same in all cultures?

_____3. According to the context of paragraph 1, the best definition of *universal* is _____.
   a. important
   b. mandatory
   c. world-wide
   d. optional

_____4. According to the context of paragraph 2, *polygyny* means _____.
   a. having more than one husband
   b. having more than one wife
   c. marrying outside one's faith
   d. marrying outside one's tribe

_____5. According to the context of paragraph 2, *polyandry* means _____.
   a. having more than one husband
   b. having more than one wife
   c. marrying outside one's faith
   d. marrying outside one's tribe

_____6. According to the context of paragraph 3, a *berdache* is a Native American _____.
   a. spouse
   b. dwelling
   c. ceremony
   d. healer

_____7. Marriage among the Banaro in New Guinea depends upon _____.
   a. the ability of the wife to have children
   b. the ability of the husband to provide for a family
   c. the amount of the dowry provided by the bride's father
   d. the approval of the new mother-in-law by the husband's family

_____8. Based on the information in paragraph 3, marriage customs _____.
   a. are the same around the word
   b. prevent same-sex marriages around the world
   c. differ around the word
   d. stem from political views

_____9. Which sentence in paragraph 3 should an effective reader highlight?
   a. And so it goes.
   b. For just about every element you might regard as essential to marriage . . .
   c. Consider the sex of the bride and groom.
   d. Although in almost every instance the bride and groom are male and female, . . .

_____10. Which one of the following sentences best summarizes this article?
   a. Families are significant to humanity.
   b. Groups around the world have different customs.
   c. We can define family as the approved group into which children are born.
   d. The concept of family is universal but is difficult to define because of differing cultural views around the world.

Name_____ Section _____ Date _____ Score (number correct) _____ x 10 = _____

Directions: Using the context clues and your knowledge of word parts, select the best definition for the word in **bold** print.

Read the excerpt "Personal Space," from a college psychology textbook. Then respond to the items that follow it.

Personal Space

To help **assert** their individuality and **maintain** a sense of personal control, human beings generally try to establish appropriate degrees of personal space. **Personal space** is the area around an individual that the person considers private and that is **enclosed** by an invisible psychological boundary. **Encroachment** on that space causes displeasure and often withdrawal.

The size of your personal space can change, depending on the situation and the people near you. For example, you may walk arm in arm with a family member, but you will avoid physical contact with a stranger. You may stand close to a friend and whisper in her ear, but you will keep a certain distance from an elevator operator or a store clerk.

Anthropologist Edward Hall suggested that personal space is a **mechanism** by which people communicate with others. He **proposed** that people **adhere** to established norms of personal space that are learned in childhood. Hall observed that the use of personal space also varies from culture to culture. In the United States, especially in suburban and rural areas, people are used to large homes and generous personal space. In Japan, on the other hand, people are used to small homes that provide little personal space. In general, Western cultures insist on a fair amount of space for people, reserving **proximity** for intimacy and close friends, while Arab and some Eastern cultures allow much smaller distances between strangers.

Of course, determining personal space is a tricky **endeavor**, and researchers are trying to sort out distance estimations for adults and children and for men and women.

—Adapted from Lefton and Brannon, *Psychology*, 8th ed., pp. 635–636.

_____ 1. **Assert** means _____.
- a. deny
- b. declare
- c. lessen
- d. increase

_____ 2. **Maintain** means _____.
- a. keep in a certain place or condition
- b. plan for future use
- c. show a cooperative spirit
- d. eliminate competition

_____3. As used in the passage, "the area around an individual that the person considers private and that is enclosed by an individual psychological boundary" is known as _____.

     a. social distance

     b. spatial zones

     c. public zone

     d. personal space

_____4. **Enclosed** means _____.

     a. surrounded

     b. subdued

     c. opened

     d. withdrawn

_____5. **Encroachment** means _____.

     a. movement

     b. confusion

     c. intrusion

     d. encounter

_____6. **Mechanism** means _____.

     a. machinery

     b. system

     c. substance

     d. means

_____7. **Proposed** means _____.

     a. promised

     b. wrote

     c. vowed

     d. suggested

_____8. **Adhere** means _____.

     a. give up

     b. change

     c. hold on to

     d. advance

_____9. **Proximity** means _____.

     a. sympathy

     b. distance

     c. nearness.

     d. failure

_____10. **Endeavor** means _____.

     a. undertaking

     b. path

     c. experiment

     d. illusion

Name _____ Section _____ Date _____ Score (number correct) _____ x 10 = _____

Objective: To determine the definitions of unfamiliar words by using context clues.

Directions: Using the context clues and your knowledge of word parts, select the best definition for the word in **bold** print.

_____1. Alison knew she was **obsessed** with her fear of failure, so she read several self-help books to learn how to stop her constant negative self-talk.
    a. hidden in a dark corner
    b. haunted by a particular thought
    c. overcome with sudden joy
    d. provided with a particular talent

_____2. People who lead a **sedentary** life—that is, those who sit all day at their jobs and then at home— are encouraged by physicians to find ways to introduce some exercise into their daily routine.
    a. consisting of a layer of rock and sand
    b. aided by an assistant
    c. privately arranged
    d. characterized by little physical activity

_____3. As the college seniors lined up for the graduation ceremony, they grew **wistful**, sharing memories of the past four years and already longing for the simple, predictable days of attending classes.
    a. full of yearning or longing for something
    b. lacking thought or care
    c. sneaking an opportunity to change plans
    d. secretly planning a new move

_____4. **Impulsive** shoppers rarely think about the consequences of making large credit card purchases.
    a. deliberately denying oneself a present
    b. planning with great preparation
    c. logically weighing the possible consequences of an action
    d. acting without thought of the future

_____5. All students are expected to **adhere** to classroom rules; for those who do not stick to the codes set by the college, there will be negative consequences.
    a. celebrate
    b. follow
    c. begin a new journey
    d. deliberately avoid punishment

____6. Although the **diminutive** speaker had to stand on a box to be seen over the lectern, the audience agreed that his ideas were anything but small.
   a. unusually tall
   b. intelligent
   c. distinguished
   d. short or small

____7. The two-year-old was **reluctant** to get his first haircut until he saw the smiling stylist dressed as a kind fairy godmother.
   a. willing and eager
   b. sensitive
   c. unwilling and resistant
   d. remarkable and superior

____8. Why is it that strange people who are rich are considered **eccentric**, but strange poor people are merely odd?
   a. sad
   b. inexpensive
   c. ordinary
   d. unusual

____9. Wearing **conventional** clothes to a job interview at a bank is highly recommended, whereas more unusual outfits are acceptable for individuals seeking jobs as entertainers and artists.
   a. having to do with a conference
   b. customary and usual
   c. unusual
   d. expensive

____10. Despite the onset of Alzheimer's disease, the patient had some good days when he was **cognizant** of his surroundings and aware of the loved ones who visited him.
   a. forgetful
   b. healthy
   c. aware
   d. angry

Name_____ Section _____ Date _____ Score (number correct) _____ x 10 = _____

A. Directions: Using the context clues and your knowledge of word parts, select the best definition for the word in **bold** print.

_____1. Myleah is not an **extrovert**, but she isn't shy around people either.
    a. out-going, show-off
    b. mean, aggressive
    c. strong-willed, domineering
    d. quiet, withdrawn

_____2. Such **conventions** as shaking hands, kissing cheeks, or bowing often differ from country to country.
    a. morals
    b. romantic gestures
    c. customs
    d. characteristics

_____3. The chemistry students **railed** bitterly about their exam because they only had one week to study five chapters.
    a. demonstrated
    b. complained
    c. championed
    d. rallied

_____4. The silence in the room as the flag was carefully folded and given to the recent widow conveyed the **gravity** of the occasion.
    a. weight
    b. pleasure
    c. seriousness
    d. buoyancy

_____5. We had to **contend**, cope, with mosquitoes, ticks, and chiggers on our camping trip to the lake.
    a. struggle
    b. eradicate
    c. count
    d. research

_____6. My aunt and uncle are **advocates** for cystic fibrosis research ever since their daughter was diagnosed with this dreadful disease.
    a. lawyers
    b. supporters
    c. scientists
    d. opponents

_____7. Although a thief, his alibi was **credible** because he was never known to lie.
     a. believable
     b. doubtful
     c. ridiculous
     d. horrible

_____8. We need an accountant who is completely scrupulous, and who will not exploit our business.
     a. sly
     b. clever
     c. trustworthy
     d. interesting

B. Directions: Use the context clues and your knowledge of word parts in the following passage to determine the best meaning of the underlined words.

In New York William Randolph Hurst bought the *New York Journal*, cut the price to a penny and added color comics. Then he stole the popular comic, "Hogan's Alley," which included a character named the Yellow Kid. The *Journal* screamed attention-grabbing headlines such as "Thigh of the Body Found," and the paper offered $1,000 for information that would convict the murderer. Critics named this sensationalism **yellow journalism** after the Yellow Kid. By 1900, about one-third of the metropolitan **dailies** were following the trend toward yellow journalism.

          —Adapted from Biagi, *Media/Impact: An Introduction to Mass Media*, 8th ed. p. 57.

_____9. The best definition of *yellow journalism* is _____.
     a. business and financial reporting
     b. factual reporting
     c. argumentative reporting
     d. emotional and exaggerated reporting

_____10. *Dailies* are _____.
     a. newspapers that are printed every day
     b. fliers announcing headlines
     c. paperboys calling out the news
     d. advertisers

Name_____ Section _____ Date _____ Score (number correct) _____ x 10 = _____

A. Directions: Using the context clues and your knowledge of word parts, select the best definition for the word in **bold** print.

_____1. Peanut, a cross between a poodle and a Chihuahua, is a **bizarre** or weird-looking dog.
    a. strange
    b. cute
    c. small
    d. ordinary

_____2. Rita is not dishonest or hypocritical; in fact, the consistency of her beliefs, words, and actions makes her highly **credible**.
    a. unbelievable
    b. amazing
    c. believable
    d. susceptible

_____3. My brother's **charisma** makes him extremely popular and influential.
    a. wealth
    b. appeal
    c. education
    d. political power

_____4. During the trial, three witnesses were asked to **attest** to the defendant's whereabouts during the time the murder took place.
    a. disprove
    b. discuss
    c. challenge
    d. confirm

_____5. Former first lady Laura Bush, as a previous teacher and librarian, is a **proponent** of literacy.
    a. rival
    b. supporter
    c. doubter
    d. judge

_____6. If a blister **ruptures**, do not remove the broken skin covering it unless the skin is dirty; wash the area with soap and water and smooth the skin flap over the tender area.
    a. appears
    b. disappears
    c. bursts
    d. explodes

B. Directions: Study the following word chart. Then match the word to its definition using word parts and context clues.

Prefix	Meaning	Root	Meaning	Suffix	Meaning
dis-	down, away	*loc*	place	*-ate*	cause
re-	again back	*pater*	father	*-al*	of, like, related to
		aster	star	*-oid*	In the form of

_____ 7. Scientists have long thought that a giant _____ collided with earth and wiped out the dinosaurs.
      a. paternal
      b. asteroid
      c. relocate
      d. dislocated

_____ 8. Family leave laws give men the right to take _____ leaves from their jobs so that they may care for and bond with their newborn children.
      a. paternal
      b. asteroid
      c. relocate
      d. dislocated

_____ 9. Large companies often expect their employees to _____ to an office in another city or state in order to move up the corporate ladder.
      a. paternal
      b. asteroid
      c. relocate
      d. dislocated

_____ 10. As Jeremy's _____ shoulder was put back in its socket by the doctor, he winced with pain.
      a. paternal
      b. asteroid
      c. relocate
      d. dislocated

Name_____ Section _____ Date _____ Score (number correct) _____ x 10 = _____

A. Directions: Using context clues and your knowledge of word parts, choose the best meaning for each of the words in **bold** type.

_____1. Exercise, proper diet, and regular medical exams may increase one's **longevity** or life span.
    a. height
    b. muscle mass
    c. length of life
    d. quality of life

_____2. Marty broke up with Marie because he said she **hampered** his ability to feel good about himself.
    a. increased
    b. blocked
    c. supported
    d. created

_____3. Some songs from the 1960s and 1970s bring back **poignant**—emotional—memories of good times from my late teenage years.
    a. bitter
    b. hurtful
    c. unlikely
    d. touching

_____4. Obesity is no longer rare among American youth. It has become alarmingly **prevalent**.
    a. uncommon
    b. purposeful
    c. overweight
    d. widespread

_____5. Because Joshua did not plan to give his speech today, he had to **improvise** his presentation.
    a. quickly create
    b. avoid giving
    c. carefully prepare
    d. accept failure for

_____6. Colin faced a **dilemma** when his car wouldn't start on the very morning he had his job interview.
    a. question
    b. solution
    c. problem
    d. benefit

_____7. Education offers people skills and knowledge and acts as a **deterrent** of crime and poverty.
     a. help
     b. something that prevents
     c. waste
     d. benefit

_____8. Ordinarily a little plump, Margaret's **gaunt** appearance shocked her family.
     a. healthy and fit
     b. happy
     c. thin and bony
     d. strong

B. Directions: Use the context clues and your knowledge of word parts in the following passage to determine the best meaning of the underlined words.

The Amazon story is <u>emblematic</u> of the e-commerce environment of the past ten years: an early period of business vision, inspiration, and experimentation, followed by the realization that establishing a successful business would not be easy. Consequently, Jeff Bezos, the creator, had to <u>retrench</u> and reevaluate his plan. The changes he made ultimately led to a more finely tuned business model that actually produces profits.

—Adapted from Laudon and Traver, *E-commerce*, 3rd ed., p. 139.

_____9. The best definition of *emblematic* is _____.
     a. representative
     b. non-characteristic
     c. unbelievable
     d. measurable

_____10. The best definition of *retrench* is _____.
     a. expand
     b. rethink
     c. walk back
     d. resist

Name_____ Section _____ Date _____ Score (number correct) _____ x 10 = _____

A. Directions: Using context clues and your knowledge of word parts, choose the best meaning for each of the words in **bold** type.

_____1. Many famous and wealthy people use their power and position for **altruistic** rather than selfish causes.
    a. sharp
    b. charitable
    c. political
    d. greedy

_____2. The vice president of the United States has the power to cast a tie-breaking vote when the Senate reaches an **impasse** on passing a bill, resolution, or law.
    a. agreement
    b. standoff
    c. dialogue
    d. amendment

_____3. The **epigraph** written on the cornerstone of the library building read, "In dedication to the vision and heart of Beverly Statton."
    a. newspaper
    b. journal
    c. inscription
    d. sculpture

_____4. Politicians pay special attention to **demographic** information such as the age, gender, and income levels of the citizens in their voting districts.
    a. statistics of the human population
    b. financial information about a city
    c. medical information about a group of people
    d. religious information about a group of citizens

_____5. Every flu season, health experts work to avoid an **epidemic** of influenza.
    a. opportunity
    b. occupation
    c. outbreak
    d. opening

_____6. Cartoonists make a living using their **graphic** skills to amuse audiences.
    a. mediocre
    b. architectural
    c. masonry
    d. drawing

31

_____7. One form of peer pressure is the act of **shunning** an individual who seems different by making that person feel isolated and alone.
   a. praising
   b. accepting
   c. rejecting
   d. insulting

_____8. Robert rarely saves his money; instead, he **squanders** every penny on entertainment and clothes.
   a. wastes
   b. saves
   c. invests
   d. consumes

B. Directions: Use the context clues and your knowledge of word parts in the following passage to determine the best meaning of the underlined words.

The ability to control behavior is important because it gives psychologists ways of helping people improve the quality of their lives. Psychologists have devised types of interventions that help people gain control over problematic aspects of their lives. People can harness psychological forces to eliminate unhealthy behaviors like smoking and initiate healthy behaviors like regular exercise. Parenting practices can help parents maintain solid bonds with their children. These are just a few examples of the broad range of circumstances in which psychologists use their knowledge to control and improve people's lives. In this respect, psychologists are a rather optimistic group; many believe that virtually any undesired behavior pattern can be modified by the proper intervention.

—Adapted from Gerrig, and Zimbardo, *Psychology and Life,* 18th ed., p. 8.

_____9. The best definition of *intervention* is _____.
   a. an action that harms
   b. an action that increases
   c. an action that antagonizes
   d. an action that changes

_____10. The best definition of *harness* is _____.
   a. utilize
   b. eliminate
   c. connect
   d. destroy

CHAPTER 3: STATED MAIN IDEAS
Lab 3.1 Practice Exercise 1

Name_____ Section _____ Date _____ Score (number correct) _____ x 10 = _____

Objective: To locate topics and stated main ideas within paragraphs.

Directions: Read the following paragraph and answer the questions that follow.

[1]Often called the "forgotten nutrient," water is essential to life. [2]Without it, you could live only about one week. [3]About 65 to 70 percent of your body weight is made up of water in the form of blood, saliva, sweat, urine, cellular fluids, and digestive enzymes. [4]In all these various forms, water helps transport nutrients, remove wastes, and regulate body temperature.

— Pruitt & Stein, *Health Styles,* 2nd ed., p. 107

_____1. The topic of the paragraph is _____.
   a.   water removes waste
   b.   the importance of water
   c.   water

_____2. The main idea of the paragraph is expressed in _____.
   a.   sentence 1
   b.   sentence 2
   c.   sentence 3
   d.   sentence 4

[1]Fear of skin cancer has given sun exposure a bad rap. [2]However, a healthy body needs short daily doses of sunlight. [3]Direct sunlight helps the body produce vitamin D, and vitamin D helps the body absorb calcium. [4]Sunlight also stimulates the body to produce two important chemicals. [5]One is serotonin, which helps stabilize your moods. [6]The other is melatonin, which helps regulate your sleep cycle.

_____3. The topic of the paragraph is _____.
   a.   sunlight
   b.   vitamin D
   c.   healthy benefits of sunlight

_____4. The main idea of the paragraph is stated in _____.
   a.   sentence 1
   b.   sentence 2
   c.   sentence 3
   d.   sentence 5

33

[1]Elizabeth Hobbs Keckley may have been born a slave in 1818, but she died a talented and free dressmaker to the elite of Washington, D.C. [2]Her skill as a dressmaker to wealthy women in St. Louis enabled her to buy freedom for herself and her son for $1,200 in 1855. [3]By 1860, she had established a dressmaking business in Washington, D.C., that attracted the capital's elite. [4]Her shop boasted a parlor, private fitting room, and upstairs workroom employing a number of seamstresses. [5]When newly elected President Lincoln arrived in the city, his wife inquired where the leading women had their wardrobes made. [6]She was told that they went to Elizabeth Keckley.

— Adapted from New York Historical Society, *Enterprising Women.*

_____5. The topic of the paragraph is _____.
    a. a dressmaking business
    b. Elizabeth Keckley
    c. a successful business woman

_____6. The main idea of this paragraph is expressed in _____.
    a. sentence 1
    b. sentence 2
    c. sentence 3
    d. sentence 5

Directions: Read the following group of ideas and then answer the questions that follow.

(A) Hemingway developed his style as a reporter for the *Kansas City Star*.
(B) Hemingway used short sentences and active, simple language.
(C) American novelist Ernest Hemingway developed a writing style that earned him the Nobel Prize in literature.

_____7. The topic of the group of sentences is _____.
    a. Nobel Prize winners
    b. Ernest Hemingway
    c. Ernest Hemingway's writing style

_____8. Statement (A) is _____.
    a. the main idea
    b. a supporting detail

_____9. Statement (B) is _____.
    a. the main idea
    b. a supporting detail

_____10. Statement (C) is _____.
    a. the main idea
    b. a supporting detail

Name_____ Section _____ Date _____ Score (number correct) _____ x 10 = _____

Objective: To determine topics and main ideas of paragraphs.

Directions: Read the passages and answer the questions that follow.

Passage A

[1]Equality for women also involves expanding educational opportunities for them. [2]In many nations, girls are discouraged from pursuing an education or kept out of school altogether. [3]Over two-thirds of the world's people who cannot read are women. [4]Furthermore, data clearly show that as women receive educational opportunities, fertility rates decline. [5]In short, education helps more women pursue careers, delay childbirth, and have a greater say in reproductive decisions.

—Adapted from Withgott and Laposata, *Essential Environment: The Science Behind the Stories*, 4th ed., p. 124.

_____1. The topic of the paragraph is _____.
   a. illiteracy
   b. educating women
   c. equality for everyone
   d. declining fertility rates

_____2. The main idea of the paragraph is stated in _____.
   a. sentence 1
   b. sentence 2
   c. sentence 3
   d. sentence 5

Passage B

1 [1]Babbling is an important part of the development of spoken language in many ways. [2]For one thing, experts have observed that infants' babbling gradually acquires some of the sound patterns of the language they are hearing—a process referred to as "learning the tune before the words." [3]At the very least, infants do seem to develop at least two such "tunes" in their babbling. [4]Babbling with a rising intonation at the end of a string of sounds seems to signal a desire for a response; a falling intonation requires no response.

2 [5]A second important thing about babbling is that when babies first start babbling, they typically babble all kinds of sounds. [6]These include some that are not part of the language they are hearing. [7]Then, the sound repertoire of infants gradually begins to shift toward the set of sounds they are listening to, with the sounds they don't hear dropping out. [8]Findings like these suggest that babbling is part of a connected developmental process that begins at birth.

3 [9]Another part of that connected developmental process appears to be a kind of gestural language that develops near the end of the first year. [10]These gestures are the first signs of expressive language—the sounds, signs, and symbols that communicate meaning. [11]Pointing is the most common gesture infants use. [12]However, it is not unusual to see a baby of this age ask for things by using a combination of gestures and sounds.

—Adapted from Boyd and Bee, The Developing Child, 13th ed., pp. 192-193.

_____3.   The topic of passage B is _____.
        a.   speech
        b.   baby talk
        c.   babbling
        d.   infant communication skills

_____4.   The central idea of the passage is expressed in the thesis statement, which is _____.
        a.   sentence 1
        b.   sentence 2
        c.   sentence 4
        d.   sentence 11

_____5.   The topic of the first paragraph is _____.
        a.   singing
        b.   spoken language
        c.   intonations
        d.   acquiring sound patterns

_____6.   The author compares a baby's acquisition of sound patterns to _____.
        a.   signaling for assistance
        b.   learning music
        c.   pointing as with a baton
        d.   developing a repertoire for a performance

_____7.   The topic of paragraph 2 is _____.
        a.   the importance of babbling
        b.   sound
        c.   the development of a sound repertoire
        d.   important findings

_____8.   The main idea of paragraph 2 is stated in _____.
        a.   sentence 5
        b.   sentence 6
        c.   sentence 7
        d.   sentence 8

_____9.   The topic of paragraph 3 is _____.
        a.   gestural language
        b.   a baby's first year
        c.   pointing
        d.   expression

_____10. The main idea of paragraph 3 is stated in _____.
        a.   sentence 9
        b.   sentence 10
        c.   sentence 11
        d.   sentence 12

Name_____ Section _____ Date _____ Score (number correct) _____ x 10 = _____

Directions: Read the following passages and answer the questions that follow.

Passage A

1 [1]Throughout its history, the United States has both welcomed immigration and feared its consequences. [2]The gates opened wide (numerically, if not in attitude) for a massive wave of immigrants in the late nineteenth and early twentieth centuries. [3]During the past twenty years, a second great wave of immigration has brought close to a million new residents to the United States each year. [4]Today, more immigrants and children of immigrants (56 million) live in the United States than at any other time in the country's history. [5]Unlike the first wave, which was almost exclusively from western Europe, the second wave is more diverse. [6]In fact, it is changing the U.S. racial-ethnic mix. [7]If current trends in immigration (and birth) persist, in a little over fifty years the "average" American will trace his or her ancestry to Africa, Asia, South America, the Pacific Islands, the Middle East—to almost anywhere but white Europe.

2 [8]As in the past, there is concern that "too many" immigrants will alter the character of the United States. [9]"Throughout the history of American immigration," write sociologists Alejandro Portés and Ruben Rumbaut, "a consistent thread has been the fear that the 'alien element' would somehow undermine the institutions of the country and would lead it down the path of disintegration and decay." [10]A widespread fear in the early 1900s was that immigrants from southern Europe, then arriving in large numbers, would bring communism with them. [11]Today, some fear that Spanish-speaking immigrants threaten the primacy of the English language. [12]In addition, the age-old fear that immigrants will take jobs away from native-born Americans remains strong. [13]Finally, minority groups that struggled for political representation fear that newer groups will gain political power at their expense.

—Henslin, *Essentials of Sociology*, 5th ed., pp. 249–50.

_____ 1. The topic of the passage is _____.
    a. Americans' conflicting attitudes about immigration
    b. immigration in the United States
    c. the first wave of immigration in the United States
    d. the second wave of immigration in the United States

_____ 2. The central idea of the passage is expressed in the thesis statement, which is _____.
    a. sentence 1
    b. sentence 2
    c. sentence 3
    d. sentence 7

_____ 3. The topic of paragraph 1 is _____.
    a. number of immigrants
    b. problems of immigration
    c. immigration
    d. average Americans

_____ 4. How many waves of immigration are discussed in paragraph 1?
   a. one
   b. two
   c. three
   d. four

_____ 5. The topic of paragraph 2 is _____.
   a. California's changing population
   b. English and Spanish as the main languages of the United States
   c. the effect of immigration on the workforce
   d. fears that some people have about the growing number of immigrants

_____ 6. The main idea of paragraph 2 is expressed in the topic sentence, which states,
   a. As in the past, there is concern that 'too many' immigrants will alter the character of the United States.
   b. A widespread fear in the early 1900s was that immigrants from southern Europe, then arriving in large numbers, would bring communism with them.
   c. Today, some fear that Spanish-speaking immigrants threaten the primacy of the English language.
   d. Finally, minority groups that struggled for political representation fear that newer groups will gain political power at their expense.

Passage B

1 Critical viewing of visual art is difficult at first. Much that is praised in contemporary painting and sculpture may look so unfamiliar that the tendency is to say, "I don't understand it," and drop the subject. Instead, stand back, look carefully at the work, be positive, and try as hard as possible to describe exactly what is there before you: "This is a large canvas, mainly white, with broad strokes of scarlet, resembling comets." The description does not say whether the painting is worth the time to investigate it, but you can never get to evaluating it without first seeing it clearly without a preset attitude.

2 The 1997 blockbuster film *Titanic* offers a good opportunity to practice the skill of noticing. Everyone knows about the disaster that befell the ship and its passengers in 1912. The climax is clear from the beginning. There can be no surprises. What interests us along the way? *Irony*, of course: the opening shots of the magnificent vessel and the champagne bottle confidently broken across the hull; the cheering of the crowd; the proud faces of owners and builders; quick scenes of a few families and couples who will be shown again as the voyage proceeds, people whose lives we know will be ended or changed forever as the ship comes closer and closer to its dread fate; a little further on, quick cuts to the telegraph operators receiving reports of icebergs; and then close-ups of bits of ice floating in the serene waters through which the ship glides, telltale signs that go unnoticed, so that, even though the ending of the film is obvious, the piling up of these details can intensify the emotions of some viewers, even those who may ultimately decide that there is too *much* irony, that the inevitable tragedy is overstated.

—Janaro & Altshuler. *The Art of Being Human*, 7th ed., pp. 25–26.

_____ 7. The topic of the passage is _____.
   a. visual art
   b. critical viewing of visual art
   c. critical viewing of painting
   d. sculpture

_____8. The author's central point about the topic is expressed in which sentence?
     a. Critical viewing of visual art is difficult at first.
     b. Much that is praised in contemporary painting and sculpture may look so unfamiliar that the tendency is to say, "I don't understand it," and drop the subject.
     c. Instead, stand back, look carefully at the work, be positive, and try as hard as possible to describe exactly what is there before you: "This is a large canvas, mainly white, with broad strokes of scarlet, resembling comets."
     d. The description does not say whether the painting is worth the time to investigate it, but you can never get to evaluating it without first seeing it clearly without a preset attitude.

_____9. The topic of paragraph 2 is _____.
     a. irony
     b. irony in film
     c. disaster films
     d. the skill of noticing as applied to irony in *Titanic*

_____10. What is the main idea of paragraph 2?
     a. *Titanic* was a blockbuster film.
     b. Details of irony in *Titanic* provide an opportunity to practice the skill of noticing.
     c. Irony is an excellent visual tool for filmmakers.
     d. The skill of noticing requires practice.

Name_____ Section _____ Date _____ Score (number correct) _____ x 10 = _____

Directions: Read the following paragraphs and answer the questions that follow.

[1]Because nicotine is habit-forming, kicking the smoking habit takes time and knowledge. [2]Half of the battle in quitting is knowing you need to quit. [3]This knowledge will help you deal better with the likely symptoms of withdrawal, such as irritability and an intense desire to smoke. [4]A number of quitting methods are available, including nicotine replacement products (gum and patches), but there is no easy way. [5]Nearly all smokers have some feelings of nicotine withdrawal when they try to quit. [6]Give yourself a month to get over these feelings. [7]Take quitting one day at a time, even one minute at a time—whatever you need to succeed.

—Adapted from the National Center for Chronic Disease Prevention and Health Promotion, "Don't Let Another Year Go Up in Smoke."

_____1. The topic of the paragraph is _____.
     a. kicking the smoking habit
     b. the smoking habit
     c. withdrawal symptoms

_____2. The main idea of the paragraph is expressed in _____.
     a. sentence 1
     b. sentence 2
     c. sentence 3
     d. sentence 4

[1]Susan is getting anxious. [2]She is applying to MBA programs and desperately wants to get into a top-ten school. [3]She believes that graduating from a high-ranked business school could make all the difference in recouping the money she will spend getting her MBA. [4]She also knows that admittance to a top program could be difficult. [5]Her friend, an executive recruiter, advises her to "spin" her previous title and experience to make herself look better. [6]Susan isn't sure if this is the right thing to do. Ethical situations like this are a challenge to many young businesspeople.

—Adapted from Wicks, Freeman, Werhane, and Martin, *Business Ethics: A Managerial Approach*, pp.1–2.

_____3. The topic of the paragraph is _____.
     a. Susan's plan for recouping educational expenses
     b. advice for applying to MBA programs
     c. ethical challenges for young businesspeople

_____4. The main idea of the paragraph is stated in _____.
     a. sentence 1
     b. sentence 2
     c. sentence 5
     d. sentence 6

[1]When you think of NASCAR, do you think of tobacco-spitting rednecks in pickup trucks at run-down racetracks? [2]Think again! [3]These days, NASCAR is a great marketing organization that focuses single-mindedly on creating customer relationships. [4]For its fans, NASCAR is a lot more than stock car races. [5]It's a high-octane, totally involving experience. [6]And it is now the second-highest rated regular season sport on TV. [7]Races are seen in 150 countries in 23 languages. [8]There are 75 million NASCAR fans and they are young, affluent, and decidedly family oriented—40 percent are women. [9]A hardcore NASCAR fan spends nearly $700 a year on NASCAR-related clothing, collectibles, ad other items.

—Adapted from Kotler and Armstrong, *Principles of Marketing*, 13th ed., p. 36.

_____5. The topic of the paragraph is _____.
    a. stock car racing
    b. NASCAR's customer relationships
    c. money spent by NASCAR fans

_____6. The main idea of this paragraph is expressed in _____.
    a. sentence 1
    b. sentence 2
    c. sentence 3
    d. sentence 5

Directions: Read the following group of ideas and then answer the questions that follow.

(a) *Law and Order* is a high-quality TV crime drama.
(b) Each week, the show thoughtfully tracks a murder through the police investigation and the trial of the person arrested as responsible for the murder.
(c) The show is entering its 14th season, won an Emmy in 1997 for outstanding drama series, and has been nominated for the award 11 years in a row.

_____7. The topic of the group of sentences is _____.
    a. murder mysteries
    b. award-winning TV dramas
    c. *Law and Order*

_____8. Statement (a) is _____.
    a. the main idea
    b. a supporting detail

_____9. Statement (b) is _____.
    a. the main idea
    b. a supporting detail

_____10. Statement (c) is _____.
    a. the main idea
    b. a supporting detail

Name _____ Section _____ Date _____ Score (number correct) _____ x 10 = _____

Directions: Read the following passages and answer the questions that follow.

Passage A

1 [1]Conflict resolution is an extremely important communication experience that can be more positive by following some conflict management stages. [2]First, try to fight in private. [3]When you air your conflicts in front of others, you create a variety of other problems. [4]You may not be willing to be totally honest when third parties are present; you may feel you have to save face and therefore must win the fight at all costs. [5]This may lead you to use strategies to win the argument rather than to resolve the conflict. [6]You may become so absorbed by the image that others will have of you that you forget you have a relationship problem that needs to be resolved. [7]Also, you run the risk of embarrassing your partner in front of others, and this embarrassment may create resentment and hostility.

2 [8]Next, examine possible solutions. [9]Most conflicts can probably be resolved through a variety of solutions. [10]Begin by brainstorming by yourself or with your partner. [11]Try not to inhibit or censor yourself or your partner as you generate these potential solutions. [12]Once you have proposed a variety of solutions, look especially for solutions that will enable each party to win—to get something he or she wants. [13]Avoid win-lose solutions, in which one person wins and one loses. [14]Such outcomes will cause difficulty for the relationship by engendering frustration and resentment. [15]Carefully weigh the costs and the rewards that each solution entails. [16]Most solutions will involve costs to one or both parties. [17]Seek solutions in which the costs and the rewards will be evenly shared.

3 [18]Then test the solution mentally. [19]How does it feel now? [20]How will it feel tomorrow? [21]Are you comfortable with it? [22]Second, test the solution in practice. [23]Put the solution into operation. [24]How does it work? [25]If it doesn't work, then discard it and try another. [26]Give each solution a fair chance, but don't hang on to one that won't resolve the conflict. [27]In short, test each solution until you find one that makes the situation better now than it was before.

—Adapted from DeVito, *The Interpersonal Communication Book*, 13th ed., pp. 298, 301.

_____1. The topic of the passage is _____.
   a. quarrels
   b. brainstorming
   c. conflict management
   d. problems

_____2. The central point of the passage is expressed in the thesis statement, which is _____.
   a. sentence 1
   b. sentence 2
   c. sentence 7
   d. sentence 27

_____3. The topic of paragraph 1 is _____.
   a. saving face
   b. fighting in private
   c. relationship problems
   d. embarrassment issues

_____ 4. The topic of paragraph 2 is _____.
   a. brainstorming
   b. censoring solutions
   c. win-lose situations
   d. examining solutions to conflicts

_____ 5. The main idea of paragraph 2 is expressed in _____.
   a. sentence 8   b. sentence 10   c. sentence 13   d. sentence 16

_____ 6. The topic of paragraph 3 is _____.
   a. mental tests
   b. testing solutions
   c. trying solutions
   d. discarding solutions

_____ 7. The main idea of paragraph 3 is expressed in _____.
   a. sentence 18   b. sentence 19   c. sentence 26   d. sentence 27

Passage B

1 [1]Some versions of an ideal bureaucracy picture a company that deliberately regulates every activity. [2]In actual organizations, however, human beings are creative (and stubborn) enough to resist bureaucratic regulation. [3]In the real world, organizations often operate with more informality. [4]Informality may amount to simply cutting corners, but it can also provide the flexibility needed to adapt and prosper. [5]In part, formality comes from the personalities of organizational leaders. [6]Studies of U.S. corporations document that the qualities and quirks of individuals—including personal charisma, interpersonal skills, and the willingness to recognize problems—can have a great effect on organizational outcomes.

2 [7]Communication offers another example of organizational informality. [8]Memos and other written communications are the formal way to spread information throughout an organization. [9]Typically, however, individuals also create informal networks that spread information quickly, if not always accurately. [10]Grapevines, using both word of mouth and e-mail, are particularly important to rank-and-file workers because higher-ups often try to keep important information from them.

—Adapted from Macionis, *Sociology,* 14th ed., pp. 154–155.

_____ 8. The central point of the passage is expressed in the thesis statement, which is _____.
   a. sentence 1
   b. sentence 2
   c. sentence 3
   d. sentence 4

_____ 9. The topic of paragraph 1 is _____.
   a. bureaucracy
   b. bureaucratic organizations
   c. organizational leaders
   d. informality in organizations

_____ 10. Which sentence states the main idea of paragraph 2?
   a. sentence 7   b. sentence 8   c. sentence 9   d. sentence 10

44

Name_____ Section _____ Date _____ Score (number correct) _____ x 10 = _____

Directions: Read the following passages and answer the questions that follow.

Paragraph A

¹Budget planning is the process of forecasting future expenses and savings. ²The first step in budget planning is to evaluate your current financial position by assessing your income, your expenses, your assets (what you own), and your liabilities (debit, or what you owe). ³Your net worth is the value of what you own minus the value of what you owe. ⁴You can measure your wealth by your net worth. ⁵As you save money you increase your assets and therefore increase your net worth. ⁶Budget planning enables you to build your net worth by setting aside part of your income to either invest in additional assets or reduce your liabilities.

—Adapted from Madura, *Personal Finance*, 3rd ed., p. 4.

1.　　The topic of the paragraph is _____.
　　　a.　assets
　　　b.　liabilities
　　　c.　assets and liabilities
　　　d.　budget planning

2.　　The main idea of the paragraph is _____.
　　　a.　sentence 1
　　　b.　sentence 2
　　　c.　sentence 3
　　　d.　sentence 4

Paragraph B

¹Advancements in technology often make it possible for us to experience historic events not only moments after they occur, but sometimes even while they occur. ²For example, images brought to us courtesy of modern technology include the horror of 9/11, the Asian tsunami of 2005, the devastation wrought by hurricane Katrina, and the May 2006 earthquake that killed thousands in Indonesia. ³We can communicate with people in almost any part of the world; we can send messages via email, fax, and telephone. ⁴We can use cameras at our computers or cell phones and visit face to face with people around the globe. ⁵We can even turn on the television and see and hear what is happening anywhere in the world or even in space.

—Adapted from Seiler and Beall, *Communication: Making Connections*. 7th ed., p. 10.

3.　　The topic of the paragraph is _____.
　　　a.　devastating events
　　　b.　mass communication
　　　c.　advances in communication technology
　　　d.　digital cameras

4. The main idea of the paragraph is _____.
   a. sentence 1
   b. sentence 2
   c. sentence 4
   d. sentence 5

Paragraph C

[1]In spite of the many challenges influencing our health, many people have made progress in reducing risks and making healthy lifestyle choices. [2]Developing and maintaining healthy habits by becoming informed consumers takes work, determination, and time. [3]Those who have achieved this goal ask more questions and learn to separate fact from fiction as they negotiate the various paths toward achieving health. [4]In addition, these individuals have identified unique ways to make small changes to sustain long-term, positive behavior change. [5]Consequently, learning to recognize unhealthy behaviors, identifying the factors that influence them, and planning the steps needed to reach personal health goals is a strategy that has worked for many in order to improve health.

—Donatelle, *Access to Health*, 10th ed., p. 4.

5. The topic of the paragraph is _____.
   a. becoming informed consumers
   b. positive behavior change
   c. healthy lifestyles
   d. strategies for improving health

6. The main idea of the paragraph is _____.
   a. sentences 1 and 5
   b. sentence 2
   c. sentence 2
   d. sentence 4

Passage D

1 [1]A Bureau of Justice study published in 2006 found that local police departments use a variety of applicant-screening methods. [2]Nearly all use personal interviews, and a large majority use basic skills tests, physical agility measurements, medical exams, drug tests, psychological evaluations and background investigations into the personal character of applicants. [3]Among departments serving 25,000 or more residents, about eight in ten use physical agility tests and written aptitude tests. [4]More than half check credit records, and about half use personality inventories and polygraph exams.

2 [5]Effective policing, however, may depend more on innate personal qualities than on educational attainment or credit history. [6]Police administrator August Volmer, one of the first people to attempt to describe the personal attributes necessary in a successful police officer, said that the public expects police officers to have "the wisdom of Solomon, the courage of David, the strength of Samson, the patience of Job, the leadership of Moses, the kindness of the Good Samaritan, the strategic training of Alexander, the faith of Daniel, the diplomacy of Lincoln, the tolerance of the Carpenter of Nazareth, and finally an intimate knowledge of every branch of the natural, biological, and social sciences."

—Adapted from Schmalleger, *Criminal Justice: A Brief Introduction*, 8th ed., p. 228.

_____7. The topic of paragraph 1 is _____.
   a. a Bureau of Justice statistics study
   b. police departments
   c. methods to screen police applicants
   d. tests that measure aptitude

_____8. The main idea of paragraph 1 is expressed in _____.
   a. sentence 1
   b. sentence 2
   c. sentence 3
   d. sentence 4

_____9. The topic of paragraph 2 is _____.
   a. police administrator August Volmer
   b. traits of effective police personnel
   c. Biblical references
   d. Educational requirements of police personnel

_____10. The topic of this passage is _____.
   a. screening methods
   b. police personnel
   c. effective personality traits
   d. identifying competent police personnel

Name_____ Section _____ Date _____ Score (number correct) _____ x 10 = _____

Objective: To determine the implied main idea by examining the supporting details.

A. Directions: Choose the best implied main idea for the following groups of supporting details.

A. Supporting details:

- Women who are pregnant should avoid drinking unpasteurized milk.
- Raw or partially cooked eggs, and raw or undercooked meat, fish or poultry may be unsafe for women who are pregnant.
- Expectant mothers should avoid certain soft cheeses such as Brie, feta, and Roquefort cheeses unless these foods are labeled as made with pasteurized milk.
- Pregnant women should avoid certain types of fish because of their high mercury content.

   —Adapted from Thompson and Manore, *Nutrition for Life*, 2nd ed., p. 346.

_____1.   Implied main idea: _____
   a.   People should avoid eating raw seafood.
   b.   Women must be careful of their diets.
   c.   Drinking unpasteurized milk can be dangerous for women who are pregnant.
   d.   A few specific foods may be unsafe for women who are pregnant.

B. Supporting details:

- We have all learned to deal with hard-to-open "childproof" packaging.
- Must drug producers and food makers now put their products in tamper-resistant packages.
- In making packaging decisions, the company must heed growing environmental concerns.
- Most companies have gone "green" by reducing their packaging and using environmentally responsible packaging materials.

   —Adapted from Kotler and Armstrong, *Principles of Marketing*, 13th ed., p.232.

_____2.   Implied main idea: _____
   a.   Children must be kept safe from both prescription and non-prescription medicines.
   b.   Safety and environmental concerns are now major packaging issues for companies.
   c.   Packaging has gone to ridiculous lengths in order to keep children safe.
   d.   Environmental concerns are an important issue for manufacturing companies.

B. Directions: Read the following paragraphs, then choose the best statement of the implied main idea for each paragraph.

Women have now become a majority of the students on college campuses across the United States. As their numbers have increased, women have become well represented in many fields of study that once excluded them, including mathematics, chemistry, and biology. But men still predominate in many fields, including engineering, physics, and philosophy. Women choose fields more in the visual and performing arts, English, foreign languages, and the social sciences. More men than women take computer science, and courses in gender studies enroll mostly women.

—Adapted from Macionis, *Sociology*, 13th ed., p. 333.

_____3. Which sentence best states the implied main idea?
    a. Gender continues to shape career choices on college campuses.
    b. More women than men are attending college.
    c. Women are now taking college courses that were traditionally once denied to them.
    d. Although more women are enrolling in college than men, they continue to be treated unfairly.

Lewis and Clark gathered a group of 48 experienced men near St. Louis during the winter of 1803-1804. In the spring, they made their way slowly up the Missouri River in a 55-foot keelboat and two dugout canoes, called pirogues. By late fall, they had reached what is now North Dakota, where they built a small station, Fort Mandan, and spent the winter. In April 1805, having shipped back to President Jackson more than 30 boxes of plants, minerals, animal skins and bones, and Indian artifacts, they struck out again toward the mountains. They were accompanied by a Shoshone woman, Sacajawea, and her husband, who acted as guides. They passed the Great Falls of the Missouri. They clambered over the Continental Divide at Lemhi Pass in southwest Montana. They descended from the Rocky Mountains to the Pacific by way of the Clearwater and Columbia Rivers. By 1806, the group had concluded its explorations of the Louisiana Purchase and returned to St. Louis.

—Adapted from Garraty & Carnes, *The American Nation,* 10th ed., p. 180.

_____4. Which sentence best states the implied main idea?
    a. Lewis and Clark spent too many months exploring the United States.
    b. From 1803 to 1806, Lewis and Clark led the exploration of the Louisiana Purchase.
    c. The United States was uncharted territory until the Lewis and Clark exploration.
    d. Lewis and Clark needed the help of guides in order to make their way over very mountainous terrain.

When Stephanie was an infant, she frequently became ill and spent a lot of her infancy in the doctor's office. Antibiotics were delivered by injections. The shots were obviously painful and caused Stephanie to scream and cry. Of course, the doctor in his white coat and the nurse in her white uniform were always present, as well as the white paper covering the examining table. It didn't take too many visits before Stephanie would scream when she saw the "white coat" people coming toward her.

—Adapted from Ciccarelli and White, *Psychology*, 2nd ed., p. 176.

_____5. Which sentence best states the implied main idea?
    a. Stephanie hated injections.
    b. Doctors and nurses should not wear white.
    c. Stephanie spent an unusual amount of time in the doctor's office when she was a baby.
    d. Stephanie learned to associate white coats and being up on a table with pain.

A credit card class refers to the credit level of the cardholder. At the low end is the standard with credit limits from $500 to $3,000. Above that are Gold cards such as the Visa Gold card, which offer a bigger line of credit, generally $5,000, and up, and provide extra perks or incentives. Finally, there are premium or prestige credit cards, such as the MasterCard Platinum card, which offer credit limits as high as $100,000 or more and benefits beyond a standard credit card, such as emergency medical and legal services, travel insurance and services, rebates, and warranties on new purchases. Now, Visa and MasterCard even offer Titanium cards, with higher credit limits and even more benefits.

> —Adapted from Keown, *Personal Finance: Turning Money into Wealth*, 5th ed., p. 171.

_____6. Which sentence best states the implied main idea?
    a. Reward programs are a gimmick that entice people to accept credit cards they don't need.
    b. There are several different classes of credit cards.
    c. Credit cards should be used for emergency situations only.
    d. Consumers should choose a credit card with the highest limits possible in order to take advantage of all the perks that come with the card.

In the United States, we say that housework is important to family life. Here, as around the world, taking care of the home and children has always been considered "women's work." As women have entered the labor force, the amount of housework women do has gone down, but the share done by women has stayed the same. Overall, women average 16.1 hours a week of housework, compared to 10.5 hours for men.
> —Adapted from Macionis, *Sociology*, 13th ed., p. 337.

_____7. Which sentence best states the implied main idea?
    a. While men may support the idea of women entering the labor force, most husbands resist taking on a more equal share of household duties.
    b. Most men believe that women should stay home and take care of the family and household duties.
    c. Men would probably do more housework if their spouses gave them more praise.
    d. Doing housework and taking care of families is the responsibility of the wife because everyone knows that women are more nurturing and do a better job at this kind of work.

On March 23, 2007, hotel Heiress Paris Hilton attended a birthday party for namesake celebrity gossip blogger Perez Hilton in West Hollywood, California. This was only two months after pleading no contest to an alcohol-related reckless driving offense in Los Angeles. Hilton was sentenced to three years' probation, fined $1500 plus court costs, and ordered to participate in an alcohol-education program. Stopped for driving with her lights out not long afterward, she was then ordered to spend time in jail—a sentence that was completed in June 2007.

> —Adapted from Schmalleger, *Criminal Justice: A Brief Introduction*, 8th ed., p. 362.

_____8.   Which sentence best states the implied main idea?
   a.   Paris Hilton is extremely wealthy.
   b.   Paris Hilton was afraid to go to jail.
   c.   Celebrities should not be subject to the same laws and fines as everyone else.
   d.   The punishment for Paris Hilton's driving offenses was minimal and did very little to teach her to obey the laws.

C. Directions: Read the following paragraph and answer the questions that follow.

The *Wall Street Journal*, the staunch advocate of capitalism, has called Karl Marx (1818-1883) one of the three greatest modern thinkers (the other two being Sigmund Freud and Albert Einstein). Marx, who came to England after being exiled from his native Germany for proposing revolution, believed that the engine of human history is **class conflict**. He said that the *bourgeoisie* (the controlling class of *capitalists,* those who own the means to produce wealth—capital, land, factories, and machines) are locked in conflict with the *proletariat* (the exploited class, the mass of workers who do not own the means of production). This bitter struggle can end only when members of the working class unite in revolution and throw off their chains of bondage. The result will be a classless society, one free of exploitation, in which people will work according to their abilities and receive according to their needs.

—Adapted from Henslin, *Essentials of Sociology*, 5th ed., p. 5.

_____9.   The topic of the passage is _____.
   a.   Wall Street's three greatest modern thinkers
   b.   Karl Marx
   c.   Karl Marx and class conflict theory
   d.   capitalism

_____10. Which sentence best states the implied main idea of the paragraph?
   a.   Karl Marx is one of the most intelligent men who have ever lived.
   b.   Karl Marx was a revolutionary leader.
   c.   Karl Marx and his theory of class conflict had a great influence on world history.
   d.   Karl Marx was considered a dangerous man in Germany because of his ideas.

Name_____ Section _____ Date _____ Score (number correct) _____ x 10 = _____

Objective: To determine the implied main ideas and central idea.

A. Directions: Read each group of supporting details. Then, choose the best implied main idea for each group.

A. Supporting details:

- You exaggerate your beloved's virtues and minimize his or her faults.
- You share emotions and experiences and speak tenderly, with an extra degree of courtesy.
- You frequently exchange messages that have meaning only within your specific relationship.
- You create and use pet names.
    —Adapted from DeVito, *The Interpersonal Communication Book*, 13th ed., p. 265-266.

____1. Implied main idea: _____
    a. People often ignore the truth about those they love.
    b. People communicate in distinctive ways when in love.
    c. People have a special way of talking to their children.
    d. People often behave foolishly when in love.

B. Supporting details:

- When applying for a mortgage loan, you may be charged an application fee by the lender.
- Lenders often charge a fee that is commonly referred to as points.
- Lenders may also charge a loan origination fee, which is usually 1% of the mortgage amount.
- An appraisal fee is charted to estimate the market value of the home and protect the financial institution's interests.

    —Adapted from Madura, *Personal Finance*, 5th ed., p.275.

____2. Implied main idea: _____
    a. The home loan application process takes a long time.
    b. Many people cannot afford to buy a home for several reasons.
    c. Loan institutions charge unfair fees when lending money for mortgages.
    d. Borrowers must pay several fees when applying for a mortgage to buy a house.

B. Directions: Read the following paragraphs; then choose the best statement of the implied main idea.

_____3. Federal legislation was passed in 1958 to regulate food additives. The Delaney Clause, also enacted in 1958, states, "No additive may be permitted if any tests show that it produces cancer when fed to man or animals or by other appropriate tests." Before a new additive can be used in food, the producer of the additive must demonstrate its safety to the FDA by submitting data on its reasonable safety. The FDA determines the additive's safety based on these data.
—Adapted from Thompson and Manore, _Nutrition for Life_, 5th ed., p.388.

    a. The Delaney Clause prevents cancer from food additives.
    b. The U.S. government attempts to regulate everything we eat.
    c. The U.S. government has taken steps to insure that food additives are safe.
    d. Most food additives are unnecessary and should be prohibited by the government.

_____4. The hormone adrenaline is released under stress and has been found to interfere with a protein that normally would suppress the growth of cancer cells. Other research has shown that stress is linked to the accumulation of genetic errors that can lead to the formation of cancer cells and tumors. Stress causes the release of hormones such as adrenaline and noradrenaline that, over time, can cause mistakes in the instructions given by the genes to the cells of the body. As these mistakes "pile up" over the years, cells can begin to grow out of control, causing the growth of tumors and possibly cancer.
—Adapted from Gerrig, and Zimbardo, _Psychology and Life,_ 18th ed., p 402.

    a. The hormone adrenaline is deadly to the human body and should be suppressed whenever possible.
    b. Nature has made many mistakes in the evolution of human beings.
    c. Most people will eventually develop cancer because of the accumulation of genetic errors over time.
    d. Stress can have a harmful effect on the body, possibly contributing to the cause of cancer.

_____5. Hippies could be found in large groups in every big city in the United States and Europe. They were so "turned off" by the modern world that they retreated from it, finding refuge in communes, drugs, and mystical religions. They were disgusted by the dishonesty and sordid antics of so many of the politicians, horrified by the brutality of Vietnam, appalled by racism, and contemptuous of the smugness they encountered in colleges and universities. Theirs was a world of folk songs and blaring acid rock music. Their slogan, "Make love, not war," was more a general pacifist pronouncement than a specific criticism of events in Vietnam. At rock concerts they listened where earlier generations had danced. Timothy Leary, a Harvard psychologist who became known as the "Johnny Appleseed of LSD," advised them to "Tune in, turn on, drop out."
—Adapted from Carnes and Garraty, _The American Nation: A History of the United States,_ 14th ed., p. 779.

    a. People in the Hippie generation became irresponsible drug addicts living on the fringes of society.
    b. Hippies were led by reckless college professors who encouraged them to use drugs and to "tune out" society.
    c. The Hippie generation withdrew from the problems of the world instead of actively working to improve them.
    d. The era of the Hippie generation was a time of disgrace and embarrassment for the United States.

_____6. India is home to 28 percent of the world's hungry people. Many of the country's people live in conditions far worse than those our society labels "poor." Shantytowns, which are clusters of huts built with branches, leaves, and pieces of discarded cardboard and tin, surround many cities. These dwellings offer little privacy and have no refrigeration, running water, or bathrooms. However, no restless young men hang out at the corner No drug dealers work the streets, and there is little danger of violence. In India, even shantytowns are organized around strong families—children, parents, and often grandparents—who often smile a welcome to a stranger.

—Adapted from Macionis, *Sociology,* 14th ed., p. 281.

   a. Life is hopeless for the poor in India.
   b. The government in India should tear down the Shantytowns and build better accommodations for the poor.
   c. India has strict rules and regulations which allow for no loitering, drug use, or violence.
   d. Poverty in India is eased by the strength and support of families.

C. Directions. Read the following passage from a college geography textbook. Identify the central idea in the space provided.

Over 200 years ago, Thomas Malthus, an economics professor, predicted that the population would always tend to increase faster than the food supply, so cycles of mass starvation would limit population increase. Since Malthus published his theory, the human population has increased from 1 billion to 6.8 billion. Today, however, there are more overweight people than undernourished people.

Since Malthus published his theory, vast prairies of North and South America, as well as food surplus regions in Australia and South Africa, have been developed. Since the 1960s, there has been a net increase of 1.2 billion acres of agricultural land that were mostly opened by irrigation.

Even before Malthus wrote, the Western Hemisphere had contributed important food crops to the Eastern Hemisphere. For example the potato is native to the Andes region of South America. It yields the second highest number of calories per acre of any crop. By Malthus's day, it had already become a major food in northern Europe. China has recently recognized the potato's versatility and is today the world's largest producer. Russia is in second place, followed by India and the United States. The crop is becoming a mainstay throughout African and Asia.

—Adapted from Dahlman, Renwick, and Bergman, *Introduction to Geography: People, Places and Environment,* 5th ed., p. 296-297.

_____7. Which sentence best states the implied main idea of the first paragraph?
   a. Thomas Malthus was able to correctly predict the future.
   b. Human population is increasing faster than the world's ability to grow food.
   c. The mass starvation predicted by Thomas Malthus has not occurred.
   d. If the population rate continues to increase as rapidly as it has in the past 200 years, the world will experience massive starvation.

_____8. Which sentence best states the implied main idea of the second paragraph?
   a.   North and South America are supplying most of the food for the rest of the world.
   b.   The climates in Australia and South Africa are too dry to grow much food.
   c.   Extensive areas of land have been developed for agricultural use after Malthus published his theory.
   d.   Farmers are developing new means of growing crops.

_____9. Which sentence best states the implied main idea of the third paragraph?
   a.   The Western Hemisphere is taking care of supplying food to the rest of the world.
   b.   The Eastern Hemisphere has just learned about growing potatoes.
   c.   The potato has become a favorite food of most people in both the Eastern and Western Hemispheres.
   d.   Food crops such as the potato have been transplanted to new areas where they have thrived.

_____10. What is the implied central idea of the passage?
   a.   The world will be facing starvation in the next 200 years.
   b.   The world has avoided starvation by increasing the food supply faster than the population increase.
   c.   Producing enough food for everyone on Earth is a significant problem.
   d.   People are becoming overweight because more and more foods such as the potato are being used as a primary food source around the world.

Name_____ Section _____ Date _____ Score (number correct) _____ x 10 = _____

A. Directions: Read each group of supporting details. Then, choose the best implied main idea for each group.

A. Supporting details:

- Create a quiet, private environment.
- Sit at eye level with the client.
- Demonstrate interest with the client's concerns.
- Maintain confidentiality.

—Adapted from Kozier and Erb, *Fundamentals of Nursing:*
Concepts, Process, and Practice, 8th ed., p. 1008.

____1. Implied main idea: _____
   a. A nurse can follow several steps to establish trust and a working relationship.
   b. Creating client trust is very difficult.
   c. It is impossible to establish a good relationship without trust.
   d. Clients concerns should be of the utmost importance.

B. Directions: Choose the best implied main idea of each paragraph.

____2. When you click onto the site rockthevote.org, you get this message: "Rock the Vote is dedicated to protecting freedom of expression and to helping young people realize and utilize their power to effect change in the civic and political lives of their communities." Rock the Vote is a blend of new politics and new media. It began in 1990 to fight censorship in the recording industry, but it quickly grew to become a campaign to register voters.

—Adapted from Folkerts & Lacy, *The Media in Your Life:*
An Introduction to Mass Communication, 2nd ed., p. 3.

   a. Rock the Vote is a Web site dedicated to young people.
   b. Rock the Vote protects freedom of expression.
   c. Rock the Vote has evolved into a political and civic Web site for young people.
   d. Rock the Vote originally was formed to fight censorship.

____3. The potential for anonymity on the Internet cloaks many criminals in legitimate-looking identities, allowing them to place fraudulent orders with online merchants. They can also steal information by intercepting e-mail or shut down e-commerce sites by using software viruses. The Internet was never designed to become a global marketplace with a billion users.

—Adapted from Laudon and Traver, *E-commerce,* 3rd ed., p. 248.

   a. There are many legitimate businesses and online sites on the Internet.
   b. The Internet has become a global commercial entity.
   c. The Internet wasn't designed with security features that prevent fraudulent activity.
   d. Spreading computer viruses should be considered a major crime.

_____ 4. Police departments often become problem identifiers in communities. The police have learned that if vacant buildings are left untended, if graffiti is tolerated, and if public order violations such as public drinking, disruptive behavior by youths, and vandalism are permitted, these will be signals to people that nobody cares about the community. This is known as the broken window syndrome.

—Adapted from Fagin, *Criminal Justice,* 2nd ed., p. 295.

    a. A community with the broken window syndrome will be more vulnerable to serious crime.

    b. Most policemen prefer to work with community problems rather than other areas of law enforcement.

    c. A broken window sends the message that people can't afford repairs.

    d. Police have more tolerance for problems in communities than for people who break the law.

_____ 5. Athletes and others use a technique known as imagined rehearsal to reach their goals. By visualizing their planned action ahead of time, they will be prepared when they put themselves to the test. For example, suppose you want to ask someone out on a date. Imagine walking together to class. Then practice in your mind and out loud exactly what you're going to say. Mentally anticipate different responses and what you will say in reaction.

—Donatelle, *Access to Health*, 10th ed., p. 29.

    a. Extensive preparation is necessary before asking someone out on a date.

    b. Most people are not success the first time they ask someone on a date.

    c. Careful mental and verbal rehearsal will greatly improve the likelihood of success.

    d. Athletes are better at reaching their goals than most people because of their training.

_____ 6. On average, women retire earlier than men, largely because family events—a husband's retirement or the need to care for an ill spouse or parent—play larger roles in their decisions. Women in or near poverty, however, are an exception. Lacking financial resources to retire, many continue working into old age. This trend is especially pronounced among women of some ethnic groups, who are more likely to have minimal retirement benefits and to be caring for other family members.

—Adapted from Berk, *Development Through the Lifespan,* 4th ed., p. 626.

    a. Retirement decisions vary with gender and ethnicity.

    b. For many, eligibility for retirement benefits may be postponed to a later age.

    c. Health factors affect retirement decisions.

    d. Women are more financially able to retire earlier than men.

_____ 7. Biologists have so far identified and named about 1.8 million species, the term used for a particular type of organism, such as *Pelecanus occidentalis*, the brown pelican. Researchers identify thousands of additional species each year. Estimates of the total number of species range from 10 million to over 200 million. How do we make sense of this much diversity?

—Campbell, Reece, Taylor, and Simon, *Biology: Concepts & Connections*, 5th ed., p. 6.

    a. Finding names for all of the new species is a constant challenge for scientists.

    b. Diversity is a characteristic of life.

    c. No one scientist could count all of the species on the earth.

    d. Biologists are the scientists who identify and name new species of life.

_____8. According to Carol Kleiman, columnist for the *Chicago Tribune* newspaper, many firms screen out candidates over the phone who do not demonstrate minimal levels of enthusiasm or communication skills. She cites David Stiefel, consultant with PeopleScout, a Chicago-based firm, who says that about 65 percent of all job candidates are screened out for those reasons. He goes on to suggest that you can successfully obtain an on-site interview on the phone by speaking in a clear, concise voice and by sounding enthusiastic about the job.

—Adapted from Seiler and Beall, *Communication: Making Connections.* 7th ed., p. 481.

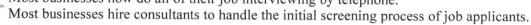

  a. Job applicants should hire a consultant in order to get through the interview process successfully.

  b. Job applicants must be prepared to handle phone interviews successfully.

  c. Most businesses now do all of their job interviewing by telephone.

  d. Most businesses hire consultants to handle the initial screening process of job applicants.

_____9. Indirect messages allow you to express a desire without insulting or offending anyone. They also allow you to observe the rules of polite interaction. So instead of saying, "I'm bored with this group," you say, "It's getting late and I have to get up early tomorrow," or you look at your watch and pretend to be surprised by the time. In each instance, you're stating a preference but are saying it indirectly so as to avoid offending someone. Sometimes indirect messages allow you to ask for compliments in a socially acceptable manner, such as saying, "I was thinking of getting my eyes done." You hope to get the desired compliment: "Your eyes? They're perfect as they are."

—Adapted from DeVito, *The Interpersonal Communication Book*, 11th ed. p. 130.

  a. Polite interaction often requires delicate handling.

  b. People often insult one another without realizing it.

  c. Indirect messages are often hypocritical—saying one thing but meaning another.

  d. Indirect messages have several advantages.

_____10. If you are far from retirement, you might consider investing your retirement contributions in mutual funds that invest in stocks with high potential for growth. This might be a capital appreciation fund, a technology fund, or maybe an international stock or bond fund. If you are close to retirement, you might consider Ginnie Mae bond funds, Treasury bond funds, or a stock mutual fund that pays high dividends. If you are young and far from retirement, you are in a position to take more risk with your investments. As you approach retirement, however, your investments should be more conservative.

—Adapted from Madura, *Personal Finance,* 3rd ed., pp. 560–561.

  a. Your retirement plan decisions should take into account the number of years until you retire.

  b. Stocks are usually considered more high risk than mutual funds.

  c. People near retirement should look for investments that will pay high dividends.

  d. Young people who are far from retirement can allow for more risk in their investment decisions.

Name_____ Section _____ Date _____ Score (number correct) _____ x 10 = _____

A. Directions: Choose the best implied main idea for the following groups of supporting details.

A. Supporting details:

- A thin, brittle, low-density layer of rock called the *crust* covers Earth's surface and rests atop a thick layer of denser rock called the *mantle*.
- The mantle surrounds a dense core consisting mostly of iron, solid in the inner core and molten in the outer core.
- A portion of the upper mantle called the *asthenosphere* contains especially soft rock, melted in some areas.
- The harder rock above the *asthenosphere* is what we know as the *lithosphere*, and this includes both the crust and the upper mantle.

—Adapted from Withgott and Brennan, *Essential Environment: The Science Behind the Stories*, 3rd ed., p. 235.

____1. Implied main idea: _____
   a. The planet Earth is composed of many layers of solid rock.
   b. The planet Earth has an unstable core that is molten.
   c. The planet Earth consists of multiple layers.
   d. The earth's crust is very thin and brittle.

B. Supporting details:

- Usually, verbal and nonverbal behaviors reinforce or support each other.
- For example, you don't usually express fear with words while the rest of your body relaxes.
- You don't normally express anger with your body posture while your face smiles.
- Your entire being works as a whole to express your thoughts and feelings.

—Adapted from DeVito, *The Interpersonal Communication Book*, 12th ed., p.99.

____2. Implied main idea: _____
   a. Both verbal and nonverbal signals occur simultaneously to express emotion.
   b. Verbal communication is the primary way we express ourselves.
   c. Fear and anger are normally expressed through nonverbal communication.
   d. Smiling is an example of nonverbal communication.

B. Directions: Read the following paragraphs, then choose the best statement of the implied main idea for each paragraph.

Simple tasks such as making hotel reservations would be nearly impossible without a credit card. Credit cards can be used as identification when cashing checks, for video rental memberships, and almost anywhere else multiple pieces of identification are needed. And using credit extends your shopping opportunities—it's nearly impossible to make a purchase over the phone or the Internet without a credit

61

card. You will receive an itemized billing of exactly how much you spent and where you spent it when shopping with a credit card. In addition, you also reduce the risk of theft associated with carrying around large amounts of cash. Finally, open credit is a source of temporary emergency funds. So, credit frees you to put your money in higher-yielding investments because you don't need to keep as much in liquid emergency funds.

—Adapted from Keown, *Personal Finance: Turning Money into Wealth*, 5th ed., p. 169.

_____ 3. Which sentence best states the implied main idea?
        a. Credit cards are an excellent source of identification.
        b. Credit cards must be kept safe because they can easily be stolen.
        c. Using credit cards will enable you to become a better investor.
        d. There are several good reasons for using a credit card in today's society.

Each year, in early March, more than 350,000 Harley bikers rumble through the streets of Daytona Beach, Florida, to attend the Daytona Bike Week celebration. Bikers from across the nation lounge on their low-slung Harleys, swap biker tales, and sport T-shirts proclaiming, "I'd rather push a Harley than drive a Honda." "You don't see people tattooing Yamaha on their bodies," observes the publisher of *American Iron*, an industry publication. And according to another industry insider, "For a lot of people, it's not that they want a motorcycle; it's that they want a Harley."

—Adapted from Kotler and Armstrong, *Principles of Marketing*, 13th ed., p. 134.

_____ 4. Which sentence best states the implied main idea?
        a. Motorcycle riders have more tattoos than most other people.
        b. The Daytona Bike Week celebration is overrun by Harley fans.
        c. Harley owners are intensely loyal to the Harley-Davidson brand.
        d. Harley Davidson motorcycles are a better bike than Yamahas or Hondas.

During the past 20 years, there has been phenomenal growth in the restaurant industry, particularly the fast-food market. During this same period, rates of obesity have increased dramatically. The portion sizes of packaged foods and restaurant meals have expanded considerably over the past 40 years. For example, the energy provided in a McDonald's lunch is enough to support an entire day's needs for a small sedentary woman. Recent studies indicate that when children and adults are presented with large portions of foods and beverages, they eat more overall and often fail to realize when they are full.

—Adapted from Thompson and Manore, *Nutrition for Life*, 2nd ed., p.271 & 276.

_____ 5. Which sentence best states the implied main idea?
        a. People who eat fast-food meals will become obese.
        b. Understanding what a healthful portion size is has become a challenging issue today.
        c. McDonald's lunches are not healthy for a normal-sized person.
        d. Obesity problems exist because of fast-food restaurants.

John F. Kennedy's death made Lyndon B. Johnson president. From 1949 until his election as vice-president, Johnson had been a senator and, for most of that time, Senate Democratic leader. He could be heavy-handed or subtle and also devious, domineering, persistent, and obliging. Many people swore by him; few had the fortitude to swear at him. Above all, he knew what to do with political power. "Some men," he said, "want power so they can strut around to 'Hail to the Chief'. . . . I wanted to use it."

Johnson, who had consciously modeled his career after that of Franklin D. Roosevelt, considered social welfare legislation his specialty. The contrast with Kennedy could not have been sharper. In his inaugural address, Kennedy had made no mention of domestic issues. Kennedy's plans for federal aid for education, urban renewal, a higher minimum wage, and medical care for the aged were blocked in Congress by Republicans and southern Democrats. The same coalition also defeated his chief economic initiative—a broad tax cut to stimulate the economy. But Kennedy had reacted to these defeats mildly, almost wistfully. He thought the machinery of the federal government was cumbersome and ineffective.

Johnson knew how to make it work. On becoming president, he pushed hard for Kennedy's programs. Early in his career Johnson had voted against a bill making lynching a federal crime, and he also had opposed bills outlawing state poll taxes and establishing the federal Fair Employment Practices Commission. But after he became an important figure in national affairs, he consistently championed racial equality. Now he made it the centerpiece of his domestic policy. "Civil righters are going to have to wear sneakers to keep up with me," he boasted. Bills long buried in committee sailed through Congress. Early in 1964 Kennedy's tax cut was passed. A few months later, an expanded version of another Kennedy proposal became law as the Civil Rights Act of 1964.

> —Carnes & Garraty, *The American Nation,* 11th ed., pp. 798–799.

_____ 6. The topic of the passage is _____.
   a. Kennedy's influence on civil rights
   b. Johnson's presidency and its effect on social reform
   c. Johnson's early career in opposition to social reform
   d. the effect of Kennedy's death on the country

_____ 7. Which sentence best states the implied main idea of the first paragraph?
   a. Lyndon B. Johnson succeeded as president after John F. Kennedy's death.
   b. Lyndon B. Johnson had been in government many years before becoming president.
   c. Lyndon B. Johnson both desired and understood how to use political power when he became president after the death of John F. Kennedy.
   d. Lyndon B. Johnson had many undesirable personality traits.

_____ 8. Which sentence best states the implied main idea of the second paragraph?
   a. President Kennedy was an ineffective leader of the United States.
   b. President Kennedy did not get along well with Congress.
   c. President Kennedy felt that the government of the United States was managed poorly.
   d. President Lyndon B. Johnson led the country in a very different way from the leadership style of President John F. Kennedy.

_____9. Which sentence best states the implied main idea of the third paragraph?
   a. President Lyndon B. Johnson successfully implemented many programs initiated by former President John F. Kennedy.
   b. Unlike former President John F. Kennedy, President Lyndon B. Johnson supported the civil rights movement.
   c. President Lyndon B. Johnson did not support federal tax cuts.
   d. Lynching was legal in the United States before President Lyndon B. Johnson outlawed it.

_____10. Which sentence best expresses the central idea of the passage?
   a. Johnson's presidency, modeled after that of Franklin Roosevelt, successfully championed many social reform issues.
   b. Kennedy was concerned about civil rights but ineffective in changing government policies.
   c. Kennedy's death was the reason civil rights reforms were effectively initiated.
   d. Johnson was a strong man, impossible to oppose and used to getting his own way.

Name_____ Section _____ Date _____ Score (number correct) _____ x 10 = _____

A. Directions: Read each group of supporting details. Then, choose the best implied main idea for each group.

Supporting details:

- Directly confronting even the idea of death is considered "morbid."
- Insurance sellers agree that life insurance is a sensitive issue.
- Married couples are urged to make out their wills as soon as the first child is born, but attorneys will tell you how seldom they do so.
- The very words "death" and "die" are considered poor taste in conversation.

—Adapted from Janaro and Altshuler, *The Art of Being Human: The Humanities as a Technique for Living,* 10th ed., p. 447.

_____1. Implied main idea: _____
   a. Insurance salesmen find life insurance a difficult product to sell.
   b. Many people don't want to face the issue of death.
   c. Society should realize that death is unstoppable.
   d. Most people are skilled at avoiding subjects they don't want to discuss.

B. Directions: Read each of the following paragraphs and choose the implied main idea.

_____2. Health problems are far greater in low-income nations than they are in the United States. The good news is that life expectancy for the world as a whole has been rising—from forty-eight years in 1950 to sixty-nine years today—and the biggest gains have occurred in poor countries. However, in much of Latin America, Asia, and especially Africa, hundreds of millions of adults and children lack not only medical attention but adequate food and safe drinking water as well.
   —Adapted from Macionis, *Sociology,* 14th ed., p. 505.

   a. The world is suffering from a multitude of problems.
   b. Improving the health of the world's poorest people is a critical challenge in the years to come.
   c. Life expectancy rates are rising everywhere except in poor countries.
   d. Much of the world is suffering from low-income.

_____3. Children watch the behavior of their parents, teachers, siblings, and even peers. A little boy sees the glory of a major league baseball player and becomes interested in sports. A little girl watchers her high-school neighbor practicing cheerleading moves and begins to try them herself. Television shows watched by children typically define female characters in terms of their relationships with males. Females are more likely appear as victims than males. They are more likely to be portrayed as characters interested in romance, their homes and their families.
   Adapted from Feldman, *Child Development,* 6th ed., p. 252.

   a. Children learn gender-related behavior and roles through observing others.
   b. Gender stereotyping in our country is having negative effects on our children.
   c. Girls learn early on that they are considered inferior to boys.
   d. Children often misunderstand the behavior of those around them and mistakenly think they should copy the behavior they see.

____4. Manufacturers claim that electronic cigarettes are a safe alternative to conventional smoking. The U.S. Food and Drug Administration analyzed samples of two popular brands of electronic cigarettes and found variable amounts of nicotine and traces of toxic chemicals, including known cancer-causing substances. Other research discovered that e-cigarette cartridges leak, which could expose nicotine to children and adults, pets, and the environment. New York is pushing to become the first state to ban these electronic devices.

—Adapted from Donatelle, *Access to Health*, 13th ed., p. 372.

    a. People shouldn't believe claims made by manufacturers.
    b. All states will soon copy New York and ban electronic cigarettes.
    c. Electronic cigarettes are not as safe as their manufacturers claim.
    d. Researchers need to provide more proof about the hazards of electronic cigarettes.

____5. Businesses give away free PCs, free data storage, free music, free Web sites, free photo storage, and free Internet connections. Free is not new: banks used to give away "free" toasters to depositors in the 1950s. Google offers free office apps, free email, and free collaboration sites. Free content can help build market awareness and can lead to sales of other follow-on products. In addition, free products and services knock out potential and actual competitors.

—Adapted from Laudon and Traver, *E-commerce*, 9th ed., p. 391.

    a. Everyone likes a bargain.
    b. Today's businesses often follow practices from
    c. Giving away free items or services is often a good business strategy.
    d. Google is a leader in paving the way for successful Internet businesses tactics.

____6. Just like individuals, species are "born", persist for some period of time, and then perish. The ultimate fate of any species is extinction, the death of the last of its members. In fact, at least 99.9% of all the species that have ever existed are now extinct. The natural course of evolution, as revealed by fossils, is continual turnover of species as new ones arise and old ones become extinct.

—Adapted from Audesirk, Audesirk, and Byers, *Biology: Life on Earth*, 10th ed., p. 305.

    a. Extinction is a natural process.
    b. Animals are becoming extinct because humans are destroying their environment.
    c. Humanity must join together and lobby to save endangered species from dying out unnaturally.
    d. Plants and animals have much in common with humans.

____7. Advertising can reach large numbers of buyers at a low cost per exposure, and it enables the seller to repeat a message many times. Nearly 111 million Americans watched the most recent Super Bowl, more than 39 million people watched at least part of the last Academy Awards broadcast, and more than 26 million fans tuned in for the kick-off of the 11th season of *American Idol*. Also, the reach of the ads was extended by millions more times through consumers who viewed them again on YouTube and company Web sites.

—Adapted from Kotler and Armstrong, *Principles of Marketing*, 15th ed., p. 421.

    a. Advertising is a must for companies in today's competitive markets.
    b. Television advertising is an effective way to reach a mass audience.
    c. YouTube and other similar Web sites are more popular sources for advertising than television.
    d. With the reach of the Internet, traditional advertising methods are now a thing of the past.

C. Directions. Read the following passage and answer the questions that follow.

Those least likely to vote are between the ages of 18 and 29 and are not in college. They do not tend to be informed about politics and current events. In comparison, persons over 65 are three times as likely to vote. According to some authorities, one reason for a low turnout for the youngest age group may have been the lowering of the voting age to 18. Young people move around more frequently than older people, and they have weaker ties to a political party because it takes time to forge such ties.

Statistics also show that the lowest economic segment of those who are eligible to vote is about one-third less likely to vote in presidential elections than the top segment. They vote even less frequently in primaries and nonpresidential elections. Of the unemployed, only one-third bothers to vote. On the other hand, the higher a person's education, the more likely that person is to vote.

—Adapted from Perry and Perry, *Contemporary Society: An Introduction to Social Science,* 13th ed., p. 438.

_____8. Which sentence best states the implied main idea of the first paragraph?
  a. Citizens in the United States between the ages of 18 and 29 are the least likely to vote in government elections.
  b. Young citizens find that the registration process in order to vote is just too cumbersome.
  c. Lowering the voting age to 18 was a bad decision that has affected the voting turnout.
  d. Building ties between young citizens and political parties is a near impossible task.

_____9. Which sentence best states the implied main idea of the second paragraph?
  a. Schools are not adequately preparing students to become voters after they graduate.
  b. Two-thirds of people who are unemployed turn out to vote in elections.
  c. Citizens between the ages of 18 and 29 probably need transportation to the polls in order to vote.
  d. There is a direct relation between the failure to vote and low socioeconomic status.

_____10. Which sentence best states the implied central idea?
  a. Providing transportation and simplifying the registration process will enable more young people to vote.
  b. Young people between the ages of 18 and 29 are too apathetic to vote.
  c. Nonvoters in the United States are young and are of lower socioeconomic status than the rest of the population.
  d. Most young people who don't vote feel that their participation in elections wouldn't make a difference in the results.

Name_____ Section _____ Date _____ Score (number correct) _____ x 10 = _____

Directions: Read each group of supporting details. Then, choose the best implied main idea for each group.

Supporting details:

- Amazon.com is a business-to-consumer site that sells consumer products to retail consumers.
- ChemConnect.com is a business-to-business exchange site that creates an electronic market for chemical producers and users.
- eBay.com is a consumer-to-consumer site that creates a market space where consumers can auction or sell goods directly to other consumers.
- Gnutella is a peer-to-peer software application that permits consumers to share music with one another directly, without intervention.

_____1. Implied main idea: _____
   a. Business-to-consumer is the most common type of e-commerce.
   b. Online markets have become very popular with consumers.
   c. There are a variety of different types of e-commerce sites.
   d. E-commerce has brought some fundamental changes in the way we do business.

_____2. Consider a word such as "death." To a doctor, this word might mean the point at which the heart stops beating. This is denotative meaning, a rather objective description of an event. To a mother whose son has just died, however, the word means much more. It recalls the son's youth, his ambitions, his family, his illness, and so on. To her, the word is emotional, subjective, and highly personal. These emotional, subjective, and personal associations are the word's connotative meanings.
                    —Adapted from DeVito, *The Interpersonal Communication Book*, 11th ed. p. 130.
   a. Words can have both denotative and connotative meanings.
   b. Denotative meanings are more objective and impersonal.
   c. Connotative meanings are subjective and highly personal.
   d. Death has many different meanings for different people.

_____3. Bombing of buildings (such as the attacks on New York and Washington on September 11, 2001, on the American embassy in Kenya in 1998; and on the World Trade Center in New York in 1993) is just one form of terrorism. Terrorism has also included bombing of ships (the USS COLE in Yemen in 2000), the assassinations of political leaders (as when Iraq attempted to kill former president George Bush in 1993), and the kidnappings of diplomats and civilians (as when Iranians took American hostages in 1979).
                    —Adapted from Edwards, Wattenberg, and Lineberry, *Government in America: People, Politics, and Policy,* 13th ed., p. 631.
   a. It is difficult to defend against terrorism, especially in an open society.
   b. Terrorists have the advantage of stealth and surprise.
   c. Terrorism can never be stopped.
   d. Terrorism takes many forms.

_____4. As you write checks, you should record them in your checkbook so that you can always determine how much money is in your account. By keeping track of your account balance, you can make sure that you stay within your limit when writing checks. This is very important because you are charged fees when you write a check that bounces. In addition, you might lose some credibility when writing bad checks, even if it is unintentional.

—Adapted from Madura, *Personal Finance,* 3rd ed., p. 125.

    a. Checking accounts allow you to draw on funds by writing checks against your account.
    b. Most people keep a checking account so that they do not have to carry much cash.
    c. You should monitor your checking account balance frequently.
    d. Writing bad checks is can get you in trouble.

_____5. Addictive exercisers abuse exercise in the same way that alcoholics abuse alcohol or addictive spenders abuse money. They use it compulsively to try to meet needs—for nurturance, intimacy, self-esteem, and self-competency—that aren't being met in more acceptable ways. As a result, addictive exercise results in negative consequences similar to those found in other addictions: alienation of family and friends, injuries from overdoing it, and a craving for more.

—Adapted from Donatelle, *Access to Health*, 10th ed., p. 363.

    a. Exercise can be addictive.
    b. Many people develop unhealthy exercise patterns.
    c. Addictions are basically all the same.
    d. Addictive exercisers often suffer from social problems.

_____6. Life originated in the sea and evolved there for almost three billion years before plants and animals began moving onto land. The evaporation of the seas provides most of Earth's rainfall, and ocean temperatures have a major effect on climate and wind patterns. Photosynthesis by marine algae and cyanobacteria supplies a substantial portion of the earth's oxygen.

—Campbell, Reece, Taylor, and Simon, *Biology: Concepts & Connections*, 5th ed., p. 690.

    a. We would not have air to breathe if it were not for our oceans.
    b. Oceans have had and continue to have an enormous impact on Earth.
    c. Much of the earth is covered by oceans.
    d. Ocean temperatures play a large role in the earth's climate and weather.

_____7. Betrayal can happen when someone trusts another person and, in one way or another, that trust is broken. For example, if you tell a friend a personal secret and especially ask for complete confidentiality and the friend then spreads the story to others, you have been betrayed. Relationships that are injured by deception and betrayal are often not repairable because of the amount of hurt such breaches of trust cause.

—Adapted from Seiler and Beall, *Communication: Making Connections.* 7th ed., p. 394.

    a. People should realize the consequences before trusting friends with secrets.
    b. Secrets are best kept to yourself.
    c. Betrayal is a warning sign that a relationship is in trouble.
    d. Friends should never reveal secrets about friends.

____8. Corporal punishment is often carried out in public so that others may witness the event. For example, in the Iranian flogging for drinking alcohol, over 1,000 people gathered in Vali-e-Asr Square in Teheran to watch the lashings. In England and the United States, hangings were once a public event, and parents brought their children to witness what happens when one breaks the law. Some advocates of general deterrence today propose that the death penalty would be a greater deterrent to crime if executions were broadcast live on television.

> —Adapted from Fagin, *Criminal Justice,* 2nd ed., p. 440.

    a. Punishments in foreign countries are far more inhumane than in the United States.
    b. Some believe that witnessing pain suffered by those who commit crimes will be a deterrent to future crimes.
    c. The death penalty has proven to be a successful deterrent to crime.
    d. Executions will be broadcast soon on television.

____9. Estimates of the prevalence of mood disorders reveal that about 21 percent of females suffer a major depression at some time in their lives compared to 13 percent of males. One factor that contributes to this difference is that on average, women experience more negative events and life stressors than men do. For example, women have a greater likelihood of experiencing physical or sexual abuse, and they are more likely to live in poverty while being the primary caregiver for children and elderly parents.

> —Adapted from Gerrig, and Zimbardo, *Psychology and Life,* 18th ed., p. 467.

    a. Women are more prone genetically to experience depression than men.
    b. Caring for elderly parents and children leads to depression.
    c. Both men and women experience negative events and life stressors.
    d. Women suffer from depression almost twice as often as men.

___10. In 1990, a 26-year-old Terri Schiavo's heart stopped briefly, temporarily cutting off oxygen to her brain. She lay in a persistent vegetative state as a result. Her husband and guardian, Michael, claimed that she had earlier told him she would not want to be kept alive artificially, but Terri's parents disagreed, and a long court case ensued. The decision to keep her alive or to remove her feeding tube bounced back and forth between the courts. Finally, 15 years later, Terri Schiavo died after her feeding tube was removed for a third time.

> —Adapted from Berk, *Development Through the Lifespan,* 4th ed., p. 650.

    a. No one should have the right to withhold treatment, permitting a patient to die.
    b. Making end-of-life decisions can involve heated controversy when the patient's wishes are unclear.
    c. The courts should never have interfered in the Terri Schiavo case.
    d. Feeding tubes should not be allowed when there is no hope for recovery.

Name_____ Section _____ Date _____ Score (number correct) _____ x 10 = _____

Objective: To identify the topic, main idea, major, and minor supporting details in a passage.

Directions: Read the following passage and answer the questions that follow.

[1]Victims and witnesses of gang violence face additional and serious problems. [2]One problem is that victims and witnesses usually live with or among the persons responsible for of the crime. [3]A second problem is that victims and witnesses often face an entire gang, as opposed to a sole attacker. [4]The gang members to blame for the violence are even likely to attend the funeral of the victim. [5]As a result, victims and witnesses are often frightened and so do not cooperate with the criminal justice system. [6]They are fearful of retaliation if they do. [7]A third major problem is that victims and survivors are often seen as contributors to the crime. [8]This is particularly true for surviving family members of murdered children, some of whom were members of gangs. [9]The belief of "contribution" leads some victim compensation programs to deny funds to victims and survivors of gang violence. [10]Victim blaming is considerable, with frequent questions being asked, for instance, "Why didn't you just move away from your gang-infested neighborhood?" or "Why was your child out, and why don't you control that child?" [11]In addition, victims are frequently afraid or unable to exercise victims' rights. [12]Because of threats, fear of retaliation, or due to poverty or culture, many victims of gang violence do not exercise their rights. [13]Another difficulty some victims face is that they are indigent and cannot afford transportation to court to exercise their right to be present. [14]Moreover some gang violence victims do not speak English and do not understand their rights or the offender's status because this information is conveyed only in English. [15]Finally, some victims simply don't trust the government.

> —Adapted from "Victims of Gang Violence: A New Frontier in Victim Services." *Victims of Gang Violence Planning Group. Department of Justice.* 25 Oct. 1996.

_____ 1. The topic of this passage is _____.
   a. the increase in gang violence
   b. victim blaming and contribution
   c. problems faced by victims and witnesses to gang violence
   d. fears of victims and witnesses to gang violence

_____ 2. Which sentence is the topic sentence that states the topic and the author's controlling point about the topic?
   a. sentence 1
   b. sentence 2
   c. sentence 3
   d. sentence 11

_____ 3. Sentence 2 serves as a _____ for the paragraph.
   a. controlling statement
   b. main idea statement
   c. major supporting detail
   d. minor supporting detail

_____4. Sentence 7 serves as a _____ for the paragraph.
   a. controlling statement
   b. main idea statement
   c. major supporting detail
   d. minor supporting detail

_____5. Sentence 8 serves as a _____ for the paragraph.
   a. controlling statement
   b. main idea statement
   c. major supporting detail
   d. minor supporting detail

_____6. Sentence 9 serves as a _____ for the paragraph.
   a. controlling statement
   b. main idea statement
   c. major supporting detail
   d. minor supporting detail

_____7. The last major detail is stated in _____.
   a. sentence 12
   b. sentence 13
   c. sentence 14
   d. sentence 15

_____8. Which of the following words or phrases in the passage indicates a list of major details?
   a. one, second, in addition, finally
   b. as a result
   c. this is particularly true
   d. because of

_____9. According to the context clues and the information in sentence 13, the word *indigent* means
      _____.
   a. uneducated
   b. poor
   c. not from the United States
   d. frightened

_____10. According to the passage, why do some victims and survivors of gang violence not receive funds from compensation programs?
   a. many don't trust the government and are afraid to ask for help
   b. many don't speak English and can't understand the requirements
   c. they are often seen as contributors to the crime
   d. they don't know how to exercise their rights

Name_____ Section _____ Date _____ Score (number correct) _____ x 10 = _____

Objective: To identify the topic, main idea, and supporting major and minor details in a textbook passage.

Directions: Read the following passage from a sociology textbook, and answer the questions that follow.

[1]The family is a social institution found in all societies that unites people in cooperative groups to care for one another, including any children. [2]Family ties are also called kinship, a social bond based on common ancestry, marriage, or adoption [3]From the point of view of any individual, families change as we grow up, leaving the family into which we were born to form a family of our own. [4]All societies contain families, but exactly whom people call their kin has varied throughout history and varies today from one culture to another.

[5]Here as in other countries, families form around marriage, a legal relationship, which comes with expectations. [6]One expectation is the traditional belief in the United States that people should marry before having children. [7]This expectation is found in the word *matrimony*, which in Latin means "the condition of motherhood." [8]Today, 59 percent of children are born to married couples, but 41 percent are born to single women who may or may not live with a partner.

[9]Families, then, have become more diverse. [10]Which relationships are and are not considered a family can have important consequences because employers typically extend benefits such as health care only to family members. [11]The U.S. Census Bureau, which collects data used by sociologists, counts as families only people living together who are linked by "birth, marriage, or adoption." [12]However, the trend in the United States is toward a broader definition of families to include couples of all genders and unmarried as well as married couples who live together. [13]These *families of affinity* are made up of people who think of themselves as a family and wish others to see them that way.

—Adapted from Macionis, *Sociology,* 14th ed. pp. 418.

_____1. The topic of the passage is
     a. social institutions
     b. marriage
     c. diversity
     d. families

_____2. The thesis statement of the passage is expressed in _____.
     a. sentence 1
     b. sentence 2
     c. sentence 3
     d. sentence 4

_____3. The topic of the second paragraph is _____.
     a. marriage
     b. matrimony
     c. traditional beliefs
     d. children

_____4. The main idea of the second paragraph is expressed in _____.
   a.   sentence 5
   b.   sentence 6
   c.   sentence 7
   d.   sentence 8

_____5. According to the passage, what percentage of children are born outside of marriage?
   a.   35 percent
   b.   41 percent
   c.   59 percent
   d.   75 percent

_____6. The term *matrimony* refers to _____.
   a.   the wedding ceremony
   b.   marriage
   c.   religious rituals
   d.   the condition of being a mother

_____7. Sentence 10 serves as a _____ for the third paragraph.
   a.   main idea
   b.   supporting detail
   c.   thesis statement
   d.   summary statement

_____8. Sentence 11 serves as a _____ for the third paragraph.
   a.   main idea
   b.   major supporting detail
   c.   introductory sentence
   d.   minor important detail

_____9. According to the paragraph, *families of affinity* are _____.
   a.   traditional families
   b.   families who are not bound together
   c.   families with only one parent
   d.   people who consider themselves a family but they may or may not be legally related

_____10. The U.S. Census Bureau is _____ about the definition of a family than what is currently accepted in America.
   a.   less flexible
   b.   more broad-minded
   c.   neutral
   d.   unrealistic

CHAPTER 5: SUPPORTING DETAILS
Lab 5.3 REVIEW TEST 1

Name_____ Section _____ Date _____ Score (number correct) _____ x 10 = _____

Directions: Read the following passage, and then answer the questions that follow.

[1]The general success of Asian Americans can be traced to three major factors: family life, educational achievement, and assimilation into mainstream culture.

[2]Of all ethnic groups, including whites, Asian American children are the most likely to grow up in a stable family. [3]They usually have two parents and are least likely to be born to a single mother. [4]Most grow up in close-knit families that stress self-discipline, thrift, and hard work. [5]This early socialization provides a strong impetus for the other two factors.

[6]The second factor is their high rate of college graduation. [7]Forty-two percent of Asian Americans complete college. [8]To realize how stunning this is, compare the statistics: 26% for white Americans, 11% for Latinos, 15% for African Americans, and 11% for Native Americans. [9]The educational achievement of Asian Americans opens doors to economic success.

[10]Assimilation, the third factor, is indicated by several measures. [11]With about two of five marrying someone of another racial-ethnic group, Asian Americans have the highest intermarriage rate of any group. [12]They also are the most likely to live in integrated neighborhoods. [13]Japanese Americans, the financially most successful Asian Americans, are the most assimilated. [14]About 73% say that their best friend is not a Japanese American.

—Adapted from Henslin, *Essentials of Sociology,* 5th ed., pp. 242, 246–247.

_____1. The topic of this passage is _____.
- a. the growing number of Asian Americans in the world
- b. the number of successful Japanese Americans in the United States
- c. the reasons behind the success of Asian Americans
- d. the percentage of Asian Americans with college degrees as compared to other ethnic groups

_____2. The central idea of the passage is stated in _____.
- a. sentence 1
- b. sentence 2
- c. sentence 5
- d. sentence 13

_____3. The main idea of the second paragraph is stated in _____.
- a. sentence 2
- b. sentence 3
- c. sentence 4
- d. sentence 5

77

_____4. How many major details support the central idea of this passage?

    a. 2
    b. 3
    c. 5
    d. 7

_____5. Which words in the passage serve as clues to the major details?

    a. *general success* and *assimilation*
    b. *of all groups* and *most*
    c. *three major factors*
    d. *several measures*

_____6. Sentence 4 serves as a _____ for the entire passage.

    a. topic
    b. main idea
    c. major detail
    d. minor detail

_____7. Sentence 6 serves as a _____ for the entire passage.

    a. topic
    b. central idea
    c. major detail
    d. minor detail

_____8. The last major detail is stated in _____.

    a. sentence 10
    b. sentence 11
    c. sentence 12
    d. sentence 14

_____9. According to the context clues and the information in the passage, *assimilation* is closely related to _____.

    a. integration
    b. socialization
    c. graduation
    d. education

_____10. Which ethnic group has the lowest rate of college graduation?

    a. Latinos
    b. African Americans
    c. Native Americans
    d. white Americans

Name_____ Section _____ Date _____ Score (number correct) _____ x 10 = _____

Directions: Read the paragraphs and answer the questions that follow.

[1]In 1996, Pan American Health Organization, an office of the World Health Organization (1996), became concerned about the rise of tuberculosis (TB) around the world. [2]Tuberculousis was then named as the world's deadliest infection due to its devastating traits and rapidly increasing incidents of the disease. [3]TB kills 3 million people (including 300,000 children) each year. [4]TB currently kills more adults each year than AIDS, malaria, and tropical diseases combined.

[5]Approximately one-third of the world's population is infected by the tuberculosis bacterium (*Mycobacterium tuberculosis*). [6]Someone in the world is newly infected with TB literally with every tick of the clock, one person per second. [7]Left untreated, one person with active TB will infect 10 to 15 people in a year's time. [8]At this rate, it is estimated that, in the next decade, 300 million more people will become infected, that 90 million people will develop the disease, and 30 million people will die from it.

[9]The infectious bacteria that cause TB lodge in the lungs and can, in time, spread to the rest of the body. [10]The TB bacilli invade and inflame the respiratory system. [11]As a result, fibrous and hardened materials encase the bacilli. [12]These encased bacilli are called *tubercles*. [13]The TB is arrested at this point, not cured. [14]This period of arrest is known as *primary tuberculosis*.

[15]When the immune system is weakened, the bacilli become active again and *secondary tuberculosis* occurs. [16]Then, extensive lesions and cavities occur in the upper portion of the lungs. [17]Over time, the following symptoms may develop: persistent coughing, weight loss, fever, night sweats, and spitting up blood (Purtilo, 1978). [18]Persons whose immune systems have been weakened by AIDS, diabetes mellitus, malnutrition, or alcoholism are more open to TB.

[19]TB is spread through the air and by casual contact. [20]When infectious people sneeze, cough, or talk, the TB bacilli in their lungs are expelled into the air where they can remain suspended for hours. [21]Then, the TB bacilli can be inhaled by others (WHO, 1996). [22]However, only 5-10 percent of people who are infected with TB actually become sick or infectious themselves, because the immune system "walls off" the TB organisms (WHO, 1996).

[23]Two major factors have contributed to the rise of TB in the United States. [24]First, the accelerated spread of human immunodeficiency virus (HIV), which leads to AIDS, increases the possibility of TB infecting the patient because of his or her weakened immune system. [25]TB and HIV form a deadly combination, each having an effect on the other. [26]The second factor is the number of new immigrants and refugees entering the United States. [27]The largest number of foreign-born people with TB originated from Mexico, the Philippines, Haiti, India, the People's Republic of China, and Vietnam. [28]In 1993, about one-fourth of reported tuberculosis cases were in people who were born outside of the United States.

—Adapted from Nakamura, Raymond A. *Health in America, a Multicultural Perspective.*
Allyn & Bacon, 1999. pp. 220–21.

_____1. The topic of this passage is _____.
  a. the rise of deadly diseases
  b. the rise and traits of tuberculosis
  c. challenges caused by the spread of deadly diseases
  d. the number of people who have succumbed to tuberculosis

_____2. Sentence 1 is a _____.
  a. controlling statement
  b. main idea statement
  c. major supporting detail
  d. minor supporting detail

_____3. Sentence 2 serves as a _____ for the paragraph.
  a. controlling statement
  b. contrasting statement
  c. major supporting detail
  d. minor supporting detail

_____4. Sentence 7 serves as a _____ for the paragraph.
  a. controlling statement
  b. main idea statement
  c. major supporting detail
  d. minor supporting detail

_____5. Sentence 8 serves as a _____ for the paragraph.
  a. controlling statement
  b. main idea statement
  c. major supporting detail
  d. minor supporting detail

_____6. Sentence 9 serves as a _____ for the paragraph.
  a. controlling statement
  b. main idea statement
  c. major supporting detail
  d. minor supporting detail

_____7. Sentence 23 serves as a _____ for the paragraph.
  a. controlling statement
  b. main idea statement
  c. major supporting detail
  d. minor supporting detail

_____8. Sentence 24 serves as a _____ for the paragraph.
  a. controlling statement
  b. main idea statement
  c. major supporting detail
  d. minor supporting detail

_____9.   Which of the following words or phrases in the last paragraph indicates the major details?
    a.   two major factors
    b.   which leads to
    c.   *having an effect*
    d.   first and second

_____10. According to the context clues and the information in sentences 11 and 12, *encase* means _____.
    a.   surround
    b.   break up
    c.   destroy
    d.   make up

Name_____ Section _____ Date _____ Score (number correct) _____ x 10 = _____

Directions: Read the paragraph, and answer the questions.

[1]Immunizations against widespread infectious diseases are one of the greatest public health success stories of all time. [2]In fact, most people have never seen or heard of anyone having the diseases such as smallpox that once wiped out entire populations. [3]Today, fear of the old "killer" diseases has waned and been replaced with distrust of the vaccines themselves.

[4]How serious a problem is this? [5]A general trend of avoiding vaccinations is growing. [6]Undervaccination rates are particularly high in college-educated white families with incomes about $75,000 a year. [7]For example, in some communities, such as Ashland, Oregon, up to 25 percent of kindergartners' parents opted their children out of at least one vaccine last year. [8]In other U.S. school districts and counties, these rates are even higher.

[9]Many parents are worried that these vaccines will cause worse problems than the disease they were designed to prevent. [10]The vaccine concerns receiving the most attention include fear that the measles, mumps, rubella vaccine can lead to autism. [11]Also, some parents fear that the B vaccine is related to multiple sclerosis. [12]In addition, some fear that the combined tetanus-diphtheria-pertussis vaccine can cause sudden infant death syndrome.

[13]Are these concerns valid? [14]Research is ongoing, but the Center for Disease Control and Prevention has found no evidence for any of these claims. [15]Much of the initial anxiety over the rubella vaccine was fueled by an article in the medical journal *The Lancet* in 1998 linking the vaccine to increased risk of autism and bowel disease. [16]The article prompted many to refuse the vaccine in the United States and elsewhere. [17]The resulting drop-off in immunizations led to increased cases of measles in many parts of the world. [18]Over 10 years later, after a thorough investigation, *The Lancet* retracted the article as being false.

—Adapted from Donatelle, *Access to Health*, 13th ed., p. 419.

_____1. The topic of this paragraph is _____.
    a. vaccines
    b. vaccination safety
    c. health issues for children
    d. how fears spread

_____2. Which sentence is the thesis statement that states the topic and the author's controlling point?
    a. sentence 1
    b. sentence 2
    c. sentence 3
    d. sentence 13

_____3. Sentence 5 serves as a _____for the paragraph.
    a. main idea
    b. major supporting detail
    c. minor supporting detail
    d. central idea

_____4. Sentence 6 serves as a _____ for the paragraph.
   a. main idea
   b. major supporting detail
   c. minor supporting detail
   d. topic

_____5. Sentence 7 serves as a _____ for the paragraph.
   a. main idea
   b. major supporting detail
   c. minor supporting detail
   d. summarizing sentence

_____6. Sentence 9 serves as a _____ for the paragraph.
   a. main idea
   b. major supporting detail
   c. minor supporting detail
   d. concluding sentence

_____7. How many major supporting details are in the third paragraph?
   a. 1
   b. 2
   c. 3
   d. 4 or more

_____8. Which words or phrase in the third paragraph signal major supporting details?
   a. *worry*
   b. *lead to*
   c. *can cause*
   d. *also; in addition*

_____9. Which sentence serves as the topic sentence in the last paragraph?
   a. sentence 13
   b. sentence 14
   c. sentence 15
   d. sentence 18

_____10. Which of the following statements is supported by the information in this passage?
   a. Parents should opt out of vaccinations for their children.
   b. Parents should wait for their children to become older before having them vaccinated.
   c. Parents should have their children vaccinated.
   d. Low-income parents will probably not have their children vaccinated.

Name_____ Section _____ Date _____ Score (number correct) _____ x 10 = _____

Directions: Read the paragraph, and answer the questions that follow.

[1]Most of these issues of science and society also involve technology. [2]Science and technology are interdependent, but their basic goals differ. [3]The goal of science is to understand natural phenomena. [4]In contrast, the goal of technology is generally to apply scientific knowledge for some specific purpose.

[5]The potent combination of science and technology has dramatic effects on society. [6]For example, discovery of the structure of DNA by James D. Watson and Francis Crick some 50 years ago and subsequent achievements in DNA science have led to the many technologies of DNA engineering that are transforming many fields including medicine, agriculture, and forensics (DNA fingerprinting, for example).

[7]Technology has improved our standard of living in many ways, but not without consequences. [8]One consequence is that technology that keeps people healthier has enabled the Earth's population to grow more than tenfold in the past three centuries, to double to over six billion in just the past 40 years. [9]The environmental effects of this growth can be devastating. [10]Global warming, toxic wastes, acid rain, deforestation, nuclear accidents, and extinction of species are just some of the repercussions of more and more people wielding more and more technology.

[11]Science can help us identify such problems and provide insight into which course of action may prevent further damage. [12]But solutions to these problems have as much to do with politics, and economic and cultural values as with science and technology. [13]Now that science and technology have become such powerful aspects of society, every thoughtful citizen has a responsibility to develop a reasonable amount of scientific literacy.

—Campbell, Reece, Taylor, and Simon,
Biology: Concepts & Connections, 5th ed., p. 12.

_____1. The topic of this passage is _____.
    a. science
    b. technology
    c. environmental effects of technology
    d. the aspects of science and technology

_____2. The controlling idea of the passage is expressed in _____.
    a. sentence 1
    b. sentence 5
    c. sentence 8
    d. sentence 11

_____3. Which sentence states the main idea in the first paragraph?
   a. sentence 1
   b. sentence 2
   c. sentence 3
   d. sentence 4

_____4. The words *for example* in sentence 6 indicate that this sentence serves as a _____ for the paragraph.
   a. topic
   b. main idea
   c. supporting detail
   d. central idea

_____5. Sentence 8 serves as a _____ for the second paragraph.
   a. major supporting detail
   b. minor supporting detail
   c. main idea sentence
   d. topic

_____6. The main idea of paragraph 3 is expressed in _____.
   a. sentence 7
   b. sentence 8
   c. sentence 9
   d. sentence 10

_____7. Sentence 8 serves as a _____ for the third paragraph.
   a. topic
   b. main idea
   c. major supporting detail
   d. minor supporting detail

_____8. According to the article, some of the benefits of technology and science include all of the following *except* _____.
   a. advances in DNA engineering
   b. advances in medicine
   c. advances in forensics
   d. limiting the world population

_____9. Some of the harmful effects of technology and science include all of the following *except* _____.
   a. global warming
   b. preserving species
   c. toxic wastes
   d. deforestation

_____10. This article suggests that the responsibility for solving the problems concerning science and technology rests with _____.
   a. every citizen
   b. the government
   c. the field of science
   d. the field of technology

Name_____ Section _____ Date _____ Score (number correct) _____ x 10 = _____

Objective: To outline major and minor details that support the central idea.

Directions: Read the paragraphs and answer the questions that follow.

[1]We spend much of lives within the collectivities that sociologists call social groups and formal organizations. [2]One important element of group dynamics is leadership. [3]Though a small circle of friends may have no leader at all, most large secondary groups place leaders in a formal chain of command.

[4]Groups typically benefit from two kinds of leadership. [5]Instrumental leadership refers to group leadership that focuses on the completion of tasks. [6]Members look to instrumental leaders to make plans, give orders, and get things done. [7]Expressive leadership, by contrast, is group leadership that focuses on the group's well-being. [8]Expressive leaders take less interest in achieving goals than in raising group morale and minimizing tension and conflict among members.

—Adapted from Macionis, Sociology, 14th ed., p. 148

____1. The central idea of the passage is stated in _____.
    a. sentence 1
    b. sentence 2
    c. sentence 3
    d. sentence 4

____2. The central idea is supported by _____.
    a. arguments against group leadership
    b. examples of groups
    c. comparisons between types of leadership
    d. effects of leadership decisions

____3. Sentence 4 serves as _____.
    a. the topic of the entire passage
    b. the central idea of the entire passage
    c. the main idea of the second paragraph
    d. a minor detail supporting the first major point

____4. Sentence 5 serves as a _____.
    a. the central idea of the passage
    b. the main idea of the second paragraph
    c. a major detail supporting the second paragraph
    d. a minor detail supporting the second paragraph

____5. Sentence 6 serves as _____.
    a. the central idea of the passage
    b. the main idea of the third paragraph
    c. a major detail supporting the third paragraph
    d. a minor detail supporting the third paragraph

____6. The phrase that signals comparisons in this passage is _____.
   a. *one important element*
   b. *two kinds*
   c. *by contrast*
   d. *Because they*

____7. Which of the following sentences serves as a minor detail supporting a major point?
   a. sentence 1
   b. sentence 2
   c. sentence 4
   d. sentence 6

8–10. Fill in the outline by completing the two major details and the minor detail that are missing.

Group Leadership

   A. _____(8)_____ focuses on completion of tasks
      1. makes plans
      2. gives orders
      3. _____(9)_____

   B. Expressive leadership focuses on _____(10)_____
      1. raises group morale
      2. minimizes tension and conflict

Lab 6.2 Practice Exercise 2

Name _____ Section _____ Date _____ Score (number correct) _____ x 10 = _____

Objective: To map the major and minor details supporting a central idea.

Directions: Fill in the concept map with supporting details from the passage.

Passage A

¹Cultural factors affect our food choices and eating patterns in several ways. ²First of all, the customs of many cultures put food at the center of celebrations of festivals and holidays, and overeating is encouraged. A second factor is that both parents now work outside the home in most American families. Consequently, more people are now embracing the "fast-food" culture, preferring and almost exclusively choosing highly processed and highly caloric fast foods from restaurants and grocery stores. Finally, coinciding with these cultural influences on food intake are cultural factors that promote an inactive life. Research with sedentary ethnic minority women in the United States indicates that there are some common barriers to a more active lifestyle. These include lack of personal motivation, lack of role models who are physically active, acceptance of larger body size, the viewpoint that exercise is culturally unacceptable, and fear for personal safety.

—Adapted from Thompson and Manore, *Nutrition for Life*, 2nd ed., p. 268.

_____ 1. The best heading for a concept map of this paragraph is _____.
   a. Factors of Culture
   b. Cultural Factors
   c. Cultural Factors That Affect Eating and Weight Gain
   d. Barriers to an Active Lifestyle

_____ 2. The major details in this paragraph are intended to _____.
   a. explain the influences of ethnic cultures
   b. list the three factors that influence food choice and eating behavior
   c. describe the problems of the fast-food industry
   d. analyze the barriers to self-motivation

3-5. Insert the details that support the central idea in the concept map below.

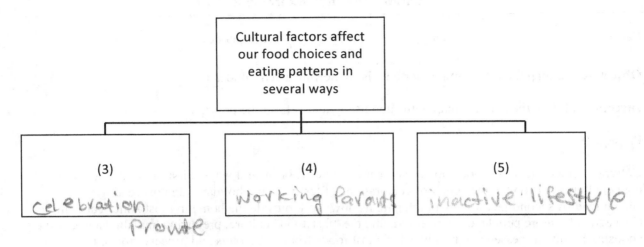

Cultural factors affect our food choices and eating patterns in several ways

(3) celebration Promte

(4) working Parents

(5) inactive lifestyle

Passage B: Several Types of Microorganisms Contaminate Foods

[1]Two types of food-borne illness are common: *food infections* result from the consumption of food containing living microorganisms, whereas *food intoxications* result from consuming food in which microorganisms have secreted poisonous substances called *toxins*. [2]The microorganisms that most commonly cause food infections are bacteria and viruses.

[3]According to the CDC, the majority of food infections are caused by **bacteria**. [4]Of the several species involved, *Campylobacter jejuni* is one of the most common culprits. [5]*Salmonella* is also a leading bacterial culprit in food infections. [6]Raw and undercooked eggs, poultry, meat, and seafood are commonly infected.

[7]The microorganisms just discussed cause illness by directly infecting and destroying body cells. [8]In contrast, some bacteria and fungi cause illness indirectly, by secreting chemicals called toxins into foods. [9]One of the most common and deadly toxins is produced by the botulism toxin. [10]Common sources of contamination are split or pierced bulging cans, food improperly canned at home, and raw honey. [11]Some fungi produce poisonous chemicals called *mycotoxins*. [12]These toxins are typically found in grains, peanuts, and other crops stored in moist environments. [13]A highly visible fungus that causes food intoxication is the poisonous mushroom. [14]Most mushrooms are not toxic, but a few, such as the "death cap" mushroom, can be fatal.

—Adapted from Thompson and Manore, *Nutrition for Life*, 2nd ed., pp. 386, 388–389.

_____ 6. Sentence 5 serves as a _____.
   a. main idea for paragraph 2
   b. major detail supporting the main idea for paragraph 2
   c. minor detail supporting a major detail for paragraph 2
   d. central idea of the passage

_____7. Sentence 6 serves as a _____.
      a. main idea for paragraph 2
      b. major detail supporting the main idea for paragraph 2
      c. minor detail supporting a major detail for paragraph 2
      d. conclusion for the paragraph

8-10. Complete the concept map by filling in the blanks.

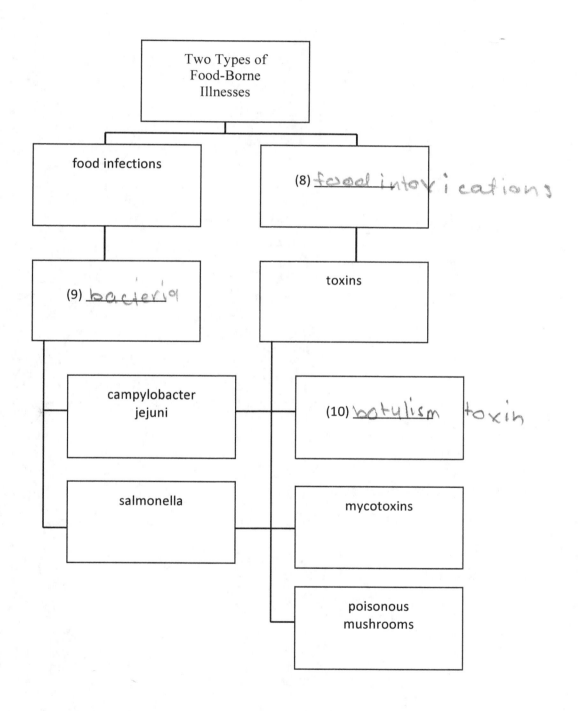

Two Types of Food-Borne Illnesses

food infections

(8) _food intoxications_

(9) _bacteria_

toxins

campylobacter jejuni

(10) _botulism toxin_

salmonella

mycotoxins

poisonous mushrooms

Name_____ Section _____ Date _____ Score (number correct) _____ x 10 = _____

Objective: To outline major and minor details that support the central idea.

Directions: Read the paragraphs and answer the questions that follow.

[1]Are you a fan of *The Weakest Link,* or do you prefer *Who Wants to Be a Millionaire?* [2]These two television shows are similar—both require participants to retrieve information that they have stored in memory. [3]They differ in rules and format, but a major difference is the way that each asks participants to access information. [4]*The Weakest Link* asks participants to recall information by reproducing it, whereas *Who Wants to Be a Millionaire?* requires participants to recognize information. [5]Psychologists use these two measures of retention, plus another method called *relearning*, to study memory.

Recall. [6]In recall tasks participants have to retrieve previously presented information. [7]Not only *The Weakest Link* but also fill-in-the-blank and essay exams require recall of information. [8]In experiments, the information usually comprises strings (lists) of digits or letters. [9]A typical study might ask participants to remember and recall ten items in a list.

[10]Three widely used recall tasks are free recall, serial recall, and paired-associate tasks. [11]In *free-recall tasks,* participants are to recall items in any order, much as you might recall the items on a grocery list. [12]*Serial-recall tasks* are more difficult; the items must be recalled in the order in which they were presented, as you would recall the digits in a telephone number. [13]In *paired-associate tasks,* participants are given a cue to help them recall the second item of a pair of items.

Recognition. [14]In a multiple-choice test, as in *Who Wants to Be a Millionaire?* you are asked to recognize information. [15]Psychologists have found that recognition tasks help them measure subtle differences in memory ability better than recall tasks. [16]That's because although a person may be unable to recall details of a previously learned fact, he or she may recognize them.

Relearning. [17]No current game show uses relearning as a memory task—it wouldn't make a very exciting show. [18]This technique assesses memory by measuring how long it takes to relearn material that a participant has learned previously. [19]The rationale for this assessment is that rapid relearning indicates some residual memory, and you can quickly relearn material because you already have some memory.

—Lefton & Brannon, *Psychology,* 8th ed. pp. 278–279.

_____1.   The topic of this passage is
   a.   *The Weakest Link*
   b.   *Who Wants to Be a Millionaire?*
   c.   recognition
   d.   retention and relearning

_____2.   The central idea of the passage is stated in _____.
   a.   sentence 1
   b.   sentence 2
   c.   sentence 3
   d.   sentence 5

_____3. The major points of this passage will most likely explain _____.
        a. how to become a participant on television game shows
        b. how to succeed in television game shows
        c. the terms used by psychologists who study memory
        d. the experiments utilized by psychologists who study memory

_____4. Sentence 10 serves as a _____ for the passage.
        a. central theme
        b. topic
        c. major detail for the passage
        d. minor supporting detail for a major detail

_____5. How many major points support the central idea of this passage?
        a. one
        b. three
        c. five
        d. seven

6–10. Fill in the outline by completing the major and minor details that are missing.

Retention and Relearning

1. (6)_____

    a. (7)_____

    b. (8)_____

    c. Paired associate tasks

    d. *The Weakest Link*, fill-in-the-blank questions, and essay tests use recall.

2. (9)_____

    a. Requires recognizing information

    b. *Who wants to Be a Millionaire?* and multi-choice tests use recognition.

3. (10)_____

    a. Measures how long it takes to relearn material

    b. Rapid relearning indicates residual memory.

Name_____ Section _____ Date _____ Score (number correct) _____ x 10 = _____

Directions: Read the paragraphs and answer the questions that follow.

[1]By the time the average infant has reached the age of 1 year, it has tripled its birth weight and added about another foot to its height. [2]The brain triples its weight in the first two years, reaching about 75 percent of its adult weight. [3]By age 5, the brain is at 90 percent of its adult weight. [4]This increase makes possible a tremendous amount of major advances in cognitive development, including the development of thinking, problem, solving, and memory.

[5]One way of examining the development of cognition is found in the work of Jean Piaget. [6]Piaget proposed that there are four distinct stages of cognitive development that occur from infancy to adolescence.

[7]The sensorimotor stage is the first of Piaget's stages. [8]It concerns infants from birth to age 2. [9]In this stage, infants use their senses and motor abilities to learn about the world around them. [10]They begin to interact deliberately with objects by grasping, pushing, tasting, and so on.

[11]Next is the preoperational stage (ages 2-7). [12]This is a time of developing language and concepts. [13]Children can now ask questions and explore their surroundings more fully. [14]However, they are not yet capable of logical thought—they can use simple mental concepts but are not able to use those concepts in a more rational, logical sense. [15]For example, it doesn't occur to them to think about how Santa Claus might get to every child's house in one night, or how he gets inside, especially when there is no chimney.

[16]In the concrete operational stage (ages 7-12), children finally become capable of conservation and reversible thinking. [17]Although children begin to think more logically and rationally, they are unable to deal effectively with abstract concepts. [18]Children at this stage need to be able to see touch, or at least see in their heads an object in order to understand it.

[19]Formal operational (ages 12 to adulthood) is the last of Piaget's stages. [20]Abstract thinking now becomes possible. [21]Teenagers not only understand concepts that have no physical reality, but also they get deeply involved in hypothetical thinking or thinking about possibilities and even impossibilities. [22]"What if everyone just got along?" [23]"If women were in charge of countries, would there be fewer wars?"

—Adapted from Ciccarelli and White, *Psychology*, 2nd ed., pp. 325–328.

_____1. The topic this passage is _____.
    a. stages of growth
    b. cognitive development
    c. tracing a life-span
    d. analyzing the thinking brain

_____2. The central idea is stated in _____.
    a. sentence 1
    b. sentence 2
    c. sentence 4
    d. sentence 6

_____3. The central idea of the passage is supported by _____.
      a. examples of cognitive abilities at each stage
      b. statistics that demonstrate differences in development
      c. testimony by noted child psychologists
      d. journal articles that confirm the information

_____4. Sentences 7, 11, 16, and 19 serve as _____.
      a. central themes
      b. main ideas
      c. major supporting details
      d. minor supporting details

_____5. Sentences 22 and 23 serve as _____ for the paragraph.
      a. central themes
      b. main ideas
      c. major supporting details
      d. minor supporting details

6-10. Fill in the outline by completing the major and minor details that are missing.

Piaget's Stages of Development

1. (6)_____

    a. Birth to 2 years of age

    b. Development of senses and motor ability

2. Preoperational stage

    a. (7)_____

    b. Development of language and concepts

    c. Lacks ability to think logically

3. (8)_____
    a. Ages 7 – 12 years of age

    b. Development of conservation and reversible thinking

    c. Lacks ability to deal effectively with abstract concepts

4. (9)_____

    a. (10) _____

    b. Development of abstract thinking

96

Name_____ Section _____ Date _____ Score (number correct) _____ x 10 = _____

Directions: Read the paragraphs and answer the questions that follow.

Paragraph A
[1]The problem of illicit drug use touches us all. [2]We may use illicit substances ourselves, watch someone we love struggle with drug abuse, or become the victim of a drug-related crime. [3]Unfortunately, illicit drug use has seen a resurgence on college campuses. [4]Research has identified several factors in a student's life that increase the risk of substance abuse. [5]The more factors there are, the greater the risk. [6]The most common reason students give to explain why they drink, smoke, or use drugs is to relax, reduce stress, or forget about problems. [7]For some students under academic and social stress, seemingly easy relief comes in the forms of drugs or alcohol. [8]A second factor is genetics. [9]Family history plays a significant role in the risk for developing an addiction. [10]The risk of drug abuse is greater if other family members have abused drugs. [11]A third factor is mental health problems. [12]Students who report being diagnosed with depression are more likely to have abused prescription drugs or to have used marijuana or other illicit drugs. [13]Being a member of a sorority or fraternity also increases the likelihood of using alcohol, marijuana, or cocaine, and makes one twice as likely to abuse prescription drugs.

—Adapted from Donatelle, *Access to Health,* 13th ed., p. 387.

_____1.   The topic of this passage is
   a.   illicit drug use
   b.   television views
   c.   television viewing habits
   d.   drug abuse on college campuses

_____2.   The central idea is the thesis statement, which is is expressed in _____.
   a.   sentence 1
   b.   sentence 2
   c.   sentence 4
   d.   sentence 5

_____3.   The major support of this passage is intended to _____.
   a. list effects of drug abuse on college campuses
   b. provide reasons that may influence drug abuse
   c. list the types of favorite drugs used on college campuses
   d. describe the studies used to measure drug abuse on college campuses

_____4.   Sentences 6, 8, 11, and 13 serve as _____ for the passage.
   a.   main ideas
   b.   major supporting details
   c.   minor supporting details
   d.   specific examples

_____5.   Which words or phrases in the passage signal a major supporting detail?
      a.   *problem*
      b.   *increase the risk*
      c.   *a second factor*
      d.   *are more likely*

_____6.   Sentence 7 serves as a _____ for the paragraph.
      a.   main idea
      b.   major supporting detail
      c.   minor supporting detail
      d.   concluding sentence

_____7.   Sentence 12 serves as a _____ for the paragraph.
      a.   contrasting thought
      b.   a main idea
      c.   major supporting detail
      d.   minor supporting detail

8–10.   Fill in the outline by completing the major and minor details that are missing.

Factors Increasing the Risk of Drug Use for a College Student

1.   Relax, reduce stress, or forget problems

2.   (8)_____

4.   (9) _____

5.   (10) _____

Name_____ Section _____ Date _____ Score (number correct) _____ x 10 = _____

Directions: Read the paragraph and answer the questions that follow.

Technological Development

[1]Technological progress begins with two factors. [2]The first factor is discovery. [3]Discovery is learning something that was not known before about the physical or social world. [4]For example, in the past, explorers have discovered new islands. [5]Astronauts have uncovered some of the laws that control the universe. [6]Invention is the second factor of technological progress. [7]An invention is a new way of doing something or a new object or mechanical device created to serve some specific purpose. [8]Inventions may be either material or nonmaterial. [9]For example, machines such as the automobile and airplane are material inventions. [10]Insurance and crop rotation are nonmaterial inventions. [11]One of the greatest of all nonmaterial inventions was the alphabet; it has made possible our present system of writing and printing.

—Adapted from Hunt & Colander, *Social Science*, 11th ed., p. 85.

_____1. The topic of this paragraph is
    a. discovery
    b. technological development
    c. great scientists
    d. inventions

_____2. The main idea of the paragraph is stated in _____.
    a. sentence 1
    b. sentence 3
    c. sentence 6
    d. sentence 11

_____3. In general, the supporting details of this paragraph _____.
    a. offer praise for explorers and inventors
    b. explain the need for funding of research
    c. explain the traits of discoveries and inventions and give examples
    d. list famous inventions

_____4. Sentence 2 serves as a _____ for the paragraph.
    a. main idea
    b. major supporting detail
    c. minor supporting detail
    d. irrelevant fact

_____5. Sentence 4 serves as a _____ for the paragraph.
    a. main idea
    b. major supporting detail
    c. minor supporting detail
    d. specific example

_____6. How many major supporting details are in this paragraph?
        a. two   b. three   c. four   d. five

_____7. What word or phrase signals the first major supporting detail?
        a. First   b. one   c. for example   d. beginning with

_____8. What word or phrase signals the second major supporting detail?
        a. And   b. next   c. second   d. for example

Directions: Use the concept map below for questions 9 and 10.

_____9. What word or phrase should complete part A of the concept map?
        a.   the first factor
        b.   discovery
        c.   laws that control the universe
        d.   technological progress

_____10. What word or phrase should complete part C of the concept map?
        a.   factor
        b.   technological progress
        c.   nonmaterial
        d.   the alphabet

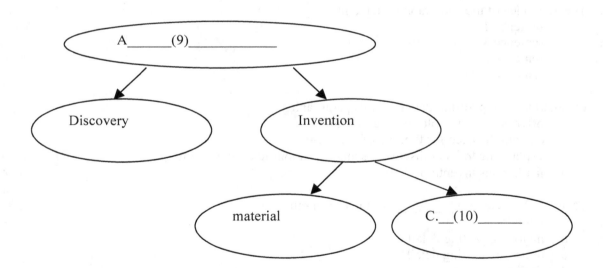

Lab 7.1 Practice Exercise 1

Name_____ Section _____ Date _____ Score (number correct) _____ x 10 = _____

Objective: To use time and space order transitions to see the relationship of details to the main idea

  A.   **Directions**: Read the paragraphs and insert the appropriate transition from the box on the numbered lines.

once	next	first	then	beginning

Check into any Ritz-Carlton hotel around the world, and you'll be amazed by the company's dedication to anticipating and meeting even your slightest need. Without ever asking, they seem to know that you want: a king-size bed, a nonallergencic pillow, and breakfast with decaffeinated coffee in your room the (____1____) morning. From the (____2____) day, those at the front desk to those in maintenance and housekeeping discreetly observe and record even the smallest guest preferences.

At the (____3____) of every morning, each hotel reviews the files of all new arrivals who have stayed previously at a Ritz-Carlton and prepares a list of suggested extra touches that might delight each guest.

And (____4____) they identify a special customer need, The Ritz-Carlton employees go to legendary extremes to meet it. For example, to serve the needs of a guest with food allergies, a Ritz-Carlton chef in Bali located special eggs and milk in a small grocery store in another country and (____5____) had them delivered to the hotel.

        —Adapted from Kotler and Armstrong, *Principles of Marketing*, 13th ed., p. 15.

B. Directions: Select the suitable transition word or expression to complete each sentence adapted from a college psychology textbook.

        —Adapted from Ciccarelli and White, *Psychology*, 2nd ed., p. 583.

_____6.   Although all people with schizophrenia share symptoms, the way in which these symptoms show up in behavior can be used to distinguish among several different _____ of schizophrenia.
     a.   spaces
     b.   times
     c.   associations
     d.   types

_____7.   There are five basic _____ of schizophrenia.
   a.   contrasts
   e.   categories
   f.   lists
   g.   additions

_____8.   One _____ of schizophrenia is *disorganized* schizophrenia. These people are very confused in speech, have vivid and frequent hallucinations, and tend to have very inappropriate emotions.
   a.   then
   b.   during
   c.   kind
   d.   behind

_____9.   Although it is becoming rare, *catatonic* schizophrenia is a _____ type of schizophrenia that involves very disturbed motor behavior. The person doesn't respond to the outside world and either doesn't move at all, maintaining often odd-looking postures for hours on end, or moves about wildly in great agitation.
   a.   previous
   b.   category
   c.   next
   d.   second

_____10.   _____, people diagnosed with *paranoid* schizophrenia suffer from hallucinations and delusions. Auditory hallucinations are common, and the delusions are typically persecution, grandeur, or extreme jealousy.
   a.   finally
   b.   then
   c.   when
   d.   another

Name_____ Section _____ Date _____ Score (number correct) _____ x 10 = _____

Directions: Read the paragraphs and answer the questions that follow.

1 Many people think of marketing as only selling and advertising. Today, marketing must be understood in the new sense of satisfying customer needs. The marketing process involves a simple, four-step model that builds strong customer relationships. As a __(1)___ step, marketers need to understand customer needs and wants and the marketplace in which they operate. __(2)___ marketing management fully understands consumers and the marketplace, they can design a customer-driven marketing strategy. The market manager must answer two important questions: *What customers will we serve?* and *How can we serve these customers best?*

2 The third __(3)___ in the process is to prepare an integrated marketing plan and program. In other words, the marketing program builds customer relationships by transforming the marketing strategy into action. The major marketing tools are classified into four broad groups, called the four Ps of marketing: product, price, place, and promotion. To deliver value, the firm must __(4)___ create a need-satisfying *product*. It must __(5)___ decide how much it will charge (*price*) and how it will make the product available to target consumers (*place*). Finally, it must communicate with customers about the product and persuade them of its merits (*promotion*).

3 The first __(6)___ steps in the marketing process all lead up to the fourth and most important __(8)___: building and managing profitable customer relationships. Customer relationship management is perhaps the most important concept of modern marketing. It is the overall __(9)___ of building and maintaining profitable customer relationships by delivering superior customer value and satisfaction. It deals with all aspects of acquiring, keeping, and growing customers.

—Adapted from Kotler and Armstrong, *Principles of Marketing,* 15th ed., pp. 12-13.

_____1. The transition word that best fits blank 1 in the first paragraph is _____.
    a. first
    b. often
    c. then
    d. additional

_____2. The transition word that best fits blank 2 in the first paragraph is _____.
    a. Began
    b. Often
    c. Once
    d. Next

_____3. The word that best fits blank 3 in the second paragraph is _____.
    a. idea
    b. step
    c. dilemma
    d. problem

_____4. The word that best fits blank 4 in the second paragraph is _____.
      a. two
      b. four
      c. step
      d. first

_____5. The transition word that best fits blank 5 in the second paragraph is _____.
      a. then
      b. answer
      c. step
      d. list

_____6. How many major supporting details support the main idea of the second paragraph?
      a. one
      b. two
      c. three
      d. four

_____7. The transition word that best fits blank 6 in the third paragraph is _____.
      a. one
      b. two
      c. third
      d. fourth

_____8. The transition word that best fits blank 7 in the third paragraph is _____.
      a. place
      b. step
      c. while
      d. then

_____9. The primary thought pattern used in the second paragraph _____.
      a. time order
      b. space order
      c. listing
      d. classification

_____10. The overall thought pattern used in the passage is _____.
      a. time order that show process
      b. space order
      c. listing
      d. classification

CHAPTER 7: TRANSITIONS AND THOUGHT PATTERNS
Lab 7.3 REVIEW TEST 1

Name_____ Section _____ Date _____ Score (number correct) _____ x 10 = _____

Directions: Read the paragraphs and answer the questions that follow.

Paragraph A

[1]Helen Fisher is a researcher at the American Museum of Natural History and an author on the topic of love, adultery and divorce. [2]In her studies, she has attempted to shed light on the process of falling in love. [3]According to Fisher, attraction and falling in love follow a pattern based on several factors. [4] The _____ factor in the pattern is imprinting. [5]Imprinting means that our genetic makeup and past experiences trigger a romantic reaction. [6]The next aspect of the pattern is attraction. [7]Attraction may be linked to chemicals in our bodies that produce feelings of euphoria and elation. [8]And a _____ factor is attachment. [9] Endorphins (natural opiates) cause lovers to feel peaceful, secure, and calm.

—Adapted from Donatelle, *Access to Health*, 7th ed., p. 133.

_____1. The main idea of this paragraph is expressed in _____.
    a. sentence 1
    b. sentence 2
    c. sentence 3
    d. sentence 4

_____2. The transition word that best fits the blank in sentence 4 is _____.
    a. *next*
    b. *frequently*
    c. *first*
    d. *additional*

_____3. The transition word that best fits the blank in sentence 8 is _____.
    a. *moreover*
    b. *frequently*
    c. *third*
    d. *additional*

_____4. The thought pattern used in the paragraph is _____.
    a. time order.
    b. space order
    c. listing
    d. classification

_____5. The transition words that signal the pattern of thought are _____.
    a. *in, according,* and *the*
    b. *researcher* and *author*
    c. *first, next,* and *third*
    d. *attraction* and *endorphins*

Paragraph B

[1]One group of students with special needs is often overlooked in schools: the gifted and talented. [2]A national survey found that more than one-half of all gifted students do not achieve in school at a level equal to their ability. [3]Individuals can have many _____ of gifts. [4]Some experts have defined giftedness as a combination of three basic _____. [5]One is an above-average general ability. [6]A _____ consists of a high level of creativity, and the third trait that marks a gifted student is a high level of commitment or motivation to achieve.

—Adapted from Woolfolk, *Educational Psychology*, 8th ed., pp. 122–123.

_____ 6. The main idea of this paragraph is found in _____.
  a. sentence 3
  b. sentence 4
  c. sentence 5
  d. sentence 6

_____ 7. The appropriate transition word for the blank in sentence 3 is _____.
  a. *group*
  b. *types*
  c. *second*
  d. *trait*

_____ 8. The appropriate transition word for the blank in sentence 4 is _____.
  a. *moreover*
  b. *characteristics*
  c. *stages*
  d. *kind*

_____ 9. The appropriate transition word for the blank in sentence 6 is _____.
  a. *one*
  b. *second*
  c. *in addition*
  d. *and*

_____ 10. The primary thought pattern used in this paragraph is _____
  a. time order
  b. space order
  c. listing
  d. classification

Name_____ Section _____ Date _____ Score (number correct) _____ x 10 = _____

Directions: Read the paragraphs and answer the questions that follow.

1 __(1)___ the 1970s, psychologists used the term *short-term memory* to refer to memory that lasts for less than a minute. However, in the 1970s, researchers Alan Baddeley and Graham Hitch __(2)___ to rethink short-term memory as a more complex type of brief storage they called *working memory*. Their model contains several levels that operate simultaneously to maintain information __(3)___ it is being processed. Earlier psychologists often concentrated on single memory tasks, trying to understand the various stages of how a single task was processed in the brain. But the concept of working memory goes beyond individual stages to describe the active integration of both conscious processes (such as repetition) and unconscious processes. This current model of memory emphasizes how human memory meets the demands of real-life activities such as listening to the radio while reading, and mentally calculating the sum of 74 plus 782 all at the same time.

2 The addition of new information may *interfere* with the recall of other information in working memory. Baddeley and Hitch demonstrated the limited capabilities of several components, or subsystems, of working memory by having participants recall digits while doing some other type of reasoning task. If one subsystem is given a demanding task, the performance of the others will suffer. One subsystem in working memory encodes, rehearses, and holds auditory information such as a person's name or phone number. __(4)__ subsystem is a visual-spatial scratch pad or blackboard, which stores visual and spatial information, such as the appearance and location of objects, for a brief time and then is erased to allow new information to be stored. A third subsystem is a central processing mechanism, something like an executive who balances the information flow and allows people to solve problems and make decisions. This executive controls the processing flow and adjusts it when necessary. Research shows that the type of information being processed by working memory affects the accuracy of the processing. For example, reading a passage consisting entirely of words presents different requirements from reading a passage with both words and pictures, and the central processing mechanism must make adjustments for the different types of information being processed.

3 Unlike the working memory, information about names, faces, dates, places, smells, and events is stored in relatively permanent form in *long-term memory*. ___(5)___ to the limitations of sensory and short-term storage, long-term memory is indefinite; much of it lasts a lifetime. The capacity of long-term memory also seems unlimited; the more information a person acquires, the easier it is to acquire more information. Using our filing cabinet analogy, we can say that long-term memory includes all the folders in the cabinet. And as in a filing cabinet, information can be lost ("misfiled") or unavailable for some other reason (the drawers can get stuck). Different from a filing cabinet, however, the information in human memory is active rather than passive in storage and subject to distortion—as if the memos in the folder had morphed into photographs of the office staff while in the cabinet.

—Adapted from Lefton & Brannon, *Psychology,* 8th ed., pp. 272–273.

_____1. The transition word that best fits blank 1 in the first paragraph is _____.
     a. next   b. often   c. until   d. additional

_____2. The transition word that best fits blank 2 in the first paragraph is _____.
     a. began   b. often   c. until   d. additional

_____3. The transition word that best fits blank 3 in the first paragraph is _____.
     a. began   b. often   c. until   d. while

_____4. Transition words such as *until, in the 1970s, earlier,* and *often* that appear in the first paragraph indicate _____.
     a. comparison
     b. time
     c. classification
     d. listing

_____5. The transition word that best fits blank 4 in the second paragraph is _____.
     a. Frequently
     b. Also
     c. Another
     d. Later

_____6. Transition words such as *several, one,* and *third* that appear in the second paragraph indicate _____.
     a. time order
     b. space order
     c. listing
     d. contrast

_____7. How many major supporting details support the main idea of the second paragraph?
     a. one   b. two   c. three   d. four

_____8. The transition word that best fits blank 5 in the third paragraph is _____.
     a. Frequently
     b. In contrast
     c. Another
     d. Later

_____9. Transition words such as *unlike, different from,* and *however* that appear in the third paragraph indicate _____.
     a. time order
     b. space order
     c. listing
     d. contrast

_____10. The topic of the entire passage is _____.
     a. memory
     b. short-term memory
     c. working memory
     d. conscious and unconscious processes

Name_____ Section _____ Date _____ Score (number correct) _____ x 10 = _____

Directions: Read the paragraphs and answer the questions that follow.

A. [1]Throughout history, societies have assumed a number of different forms. 2One way of classifying societies is according to their chief mode of subsistence. [3]The first group, the *hunting and gathering society*, is one of the earliest and least technologically complex forms of society. [4]This society is characterized by a small (around 40 individuals), nomadic population. [5]Another characteristic is that the group functions with technology that is uncomplicated. [6]In addition, there is little division of labor or specialization among the group members. [7]Finally, the group displays particular stress on the importance of kinship ties.

—Adapted from Perry and Perry, *Contemporary Society: An Introduction to Social Science*, 13th ed., p. 81.

_____1. The main idea of this paragraph is expressed in _____.
    a. sentence 1
    b. sentence 2
    c. sentence 3
    d. sentence 4

_____2. Which transitions signal the thought pattern of this paragraph?
    a. *throughout* and *earliest*
    b. *one* and *first*
    c. *classifying* and *characterized*
    d. *chief mode*

_____3. How many major details support the main idea in this paragraph?
    a. one   b. two   c. three   d. four

_____4. In general, the major details of this paragraph _____.
    a. list the characteristics of the society
    b. explain the reasons for classifying groups
    c. analyze the effectiveness of the society
    d. reveal the time era of the group

_____5. The transition words, *first, another, in addition*, and *finally* signal _____.
    a. time order
    b. listing
    c. space order
    d. classification

_____6. The primary thought pattern used in the paragraph is _____.
    a. time order
    b. process
    c. space order
    d. classification

Directions: Read the following paragraph from a college health textbook. Transition words are highlighted in **bold** type. Identify the type of transition for each of these words, and then answer the final question.

B. Approximately 20 percent of students **begin** smoking in college, **and** another 50 percent intensify their smoking behavior. To no one's surprise, the debate regarding tobacco-free campuses is contentious at many schools. **One** argument for banning tobacco on campuses is that the majority of college students (4 out of 5) do not smoke. Another argument is that two-thirds of students prefer to attend classes held on a smoke-free campus. A **third** reason is that one in five students say they have experienced some immediate health impact from exposure to tobacco smoke.

—Adapted from Donatelle, *Access to Health*, 13th ed., p. 360.

_____7. The transition *begin* signals _____.
   a. addition
   b. time
   c. space
   d. classification

_____8. The transition *and* signals _____.
   a. time
   b. space
   c. addition
   d. classification

_____9. The transitions *one* and *third* signal _____.
   a. addition
   b. time
   c. space
   d. classification

_____10. What is the overall thought pattern of the paragraph?
   a. listing
   b. time order
   c. space order
   d. classification

Name_____ Section _____ Date _____ Score (number correct) _____ x 10 = _____

Directions: Read the paragraphs and answer the questions that follow.

Paragraph A

[1]Special breathing techniques can decrease stress. [2]First, establish deep breathing from the diaphragm. [3]Then over a period of weeks, continue practicing deep breathing in order to reduce the number of breaths taken per minute. [4]_____ dealing with stressors, exhale, letting breath go slowly and deeply to reduce anxiety.

—Adapted from McGuigan, *Encyclopedia of Stress*, p. 37.

_____1. The relationship between sentence 2 and sentence 3 is one of
     a. time order
     b. listing
     c. space order
     d. classification

_____2. The transition that best fits the blank in sentence 4 is
     a. *After*
     b. *First*
     c. *When*
     d. *Finally*

Paragraph B

[1]Among mammals, only primates have full color vision. [2]A bull does not charge a red cape; he charges when he sees an annoying gray object being waved at him. [3]Among non-mammals, many birds and fishes also have excellent color vision; the brightly colored lure may really appeal to the fish as much as to the angler who bought it. [4]Most colors can be described in terms of three physical dimensions: wavelength, intensity, and purity. [5]_____, three perceptual dimensions, hue, brightness, and saturation, match the physical dimensions and help us describe what we see.

—Adapted from Carlson & Buskist, *Psychology: The Science of Behavior*, 5th ed., p. 175.

_____3. The relationship between sentence 2 and sentence 3 is one of
     a. time order
     b. listing
     c. space order
     d. classification

_____4. The transition that best fits the blank in sentence 5 is
     a. *Next*
     b. *Furthermore*
     c. *When*
     d. *Before*

Paragraph C

[1]When faithfully followed, these four steps should ensure mastery of the material you will face in an intermediate algebra class. [2]First, begin to study for the final exam three days to two weeks ahead of the exam. [3]Browse through each chapter, reviewing the important formulas. [4]If the textbook offers summaries and reviews, read these, too. [5]For step two, summarize all formulas on an index card and quiz yourself frequently. [6]As your third step, retake each chapter test that you took in class, assuming your instructor has returned it. [7]At this time, restudy the objectives in the text that go with each question that you missed. [8]Finally, for any remaining difficulties, see your instructor, go to a tutoring session, or join a study group.

—Adapted from Bittinger & Beecher, *Introductory and Intermediate Algebra,* 2nd ed., p. 892.

_____5. The topic of this paragraph is _____.
   a. mastery of material
   b. intermediate algebra class
   c. study tips for intermediate algebra
   d. steps for studying

_____6. The main idea is expressed in _____.
   a. sentence 1
   b. sentence 2
   c. sentence 4
   d. sentence 6

_____7. In general the main points of this paragraph _____.
   a. describe the difficulties of math classes
   b. classify the levels of math classes
   c. analyze the characteristics of students who perform poorly in math
   d. list the steps involved in mastering intermediate algebra

_____8. The relationship between sentence 6 and sentence 7 is one of _____.
   a. space order
   b. classification
   c. time order
   d. addition

_____9. The thought pattern used in the paragraph is
   a. classification
   b. listing
   c. time order
   d. space order

_____10. The transition words that signal this pattern are _____.
   a. *when faithfully follows*
   b. *these four steps*
   c. *on a regular basis*
   d. *use the chapter test*

Name_____ Section _____ Date _____ Score (number correct) _____ x 10 = _____

Objective: To use comparison and contrast transitions and thought patterns.

Directions: Choose the most appropriate transition to complete the sentence based upon the thought pattern that is expressed.

It is a struggle to learn a new culture, *for* the behaviors and ways of thinking contrast with the one already learned. This can lead to inner turmoil. *One* way to handle the conflict is to cut ties with your *first* culture. This, *however*, can create a sense of loss that is recognized only later in life.

—Henslin, *Essentials of Sociology,* 5th ed., p. 70.

_____1.   Which italicized word indicates a comparison-and-contrast pattern?
     a.   for
     b.   one
     c.   first
     d.   however

Richard Rodriguez, a literature professor and essayist, was born *in* the 1950s to working-class Mexican immigrants. Wanting their son to be successful in their adopted land, his parents named him Richard *instead of* Ricardo. *While* his English-Spanish hybrid name indicates the parents' aspirations for their son, it was *also* an omen of the conflict Richard would experience.

—Henslin, *Essentials of Sociology,* 5th ed., p. 70.

_____2.   Which italicized word indicates a comparison or a contrast?
     a.   in
     b.   instead of
     c.   while
     d.   also

Like other children of Mexican immigrants, Richard's *first* language was Spanish—a rich mother tongue that gave him his orientation to the world. *Until* the age of 5, when he began school, Richard knew only fifty words in English. He describes what happened *when* he began school:

The change came gradually but early. When I was beginning grade school, I noted to myself the fact that the classroom environment was so different in its styles and assumptions from my own family environment that survival would essentially entail a choice between both worlds. When I became a student, I was literally "remade"; neither I nor my teachers considered anything I had known before as relevant. I had to forget most of what my culture had provided, because to remember it was a disadvantage. The past and its cultural values became detachable, like a piece of clothing grown heavy on a warm day and finally put away.

—Henslin, *Essentials of Sociology,* 5th ed., p. 70.

____3. Which italicized transition word indicates a comparison or a contrast?
     a. like
     b. first
     c. until
     d. when

____4. According to Rodriguez, what was like a piece of clothing grown heavy on a warm day that was finally put away?
     a. giving up his dreams
     b. his connection to his culture
     c. learning math skills
     d. his connection to English literature

As happened to millions of immigrants before him, whose parents spoke German, Polish, Italian, and so on, learning English eroded family and class ties and ate away at his ethnic roots. For him, language and education were not simply devices that eased the transition to the dominant culture. Instead, they transformed Richard into a *pocho,* "a Mexican with gringo aspirations." They slashed at the roots that had given him life.

—Henslin, *Essentials of Sociology,* 5th ed., p. 70.

____5. From this paragraph, you could conclude that learning English _____.
     a. destroyed some of his family relationships
     b. destroyed some of his connections to the working class and Mexican culture
     c. changed his dreams
     d. All of the above

____6. Which culture does a *pocho* withdraw from?
     a. the old culture
     b. the new culture
     c. the Italian culture
     d. the American culture

To face such inner turmoil is to confront a fork in the road. Some turn one way and withdraw from the new culture—a clue that helps explain the high dropout rate of Latinos from U.S. schools. Others go in the opposite direction and, cutting ties with their family and cultural roots, wholeheartedly adopt the new culture.

—Henslin, *Essentials of Sociology,* 5th ed., p. 70.

____7. The explanation for the high dropout rate of Latinos in U.S. schools is that some Latinos choose to cut ties with _____.
     a. their family
     b. their past and their old culture
     c. their new culture
     d. their first language

Rodriguez took the second road. He excelled in his new language—so well, in fact, that he graduated from Stanford University and then became a graduate student in English at the University of California at Berkeley. He was even awarded a prestigious Fulbright fellowship to study English Renaissance literature at the British Museum.

—Henslin, *Essentials of Sociology,* 5th ed., p. 70.

_____8.   "Rodriguez took the second road" means that _____.
    a.   he cut ties with the English language
    b.   he cut ties with his new culture
    c.   he cut ties with his ethnic roots
    d.   he refused to excel in school

But the past wouldn't let Rodriguez alone. Prospective employers were impressed with his knowledge of Renaissance literature, but at job interviews they would ask if he would teach the Mexican novel in translation and be an adviser to Latino students. Rodriguez was haunted by the image of his grandmother, the warmth of the culture he had left behind, the language and thought to which he had become a stranger.

—Henslin, *Essentials of Sociology,* 5th ed., p. 70.

_____9.   The transition word *but* indicates that Richard Rodriguez _____.
    a.   returned to live permanently in Mexico
    b.   missed his Mexican roots and wanted to reconnect to his first culture
    c.   never found a job teaching English literature
    d.   returned to Mexico to work for his father

Richard Rodriguez represents millions of immigrants—not just those of Latino origin but those from other cultures, too—who want to be a part of the United States without betraying their past. They fear that to integrate into U.S. culture is to lose their roots. They are caught between two cultures, each beckoning, each offering rich rewards.

—Henslin, *Essentials of Sociology,* 5th ed., p. 70.

_____10. The author compares Rodriguez to _____.
    a.   other Latinos
    b.   other immigrants
    c.   people who fear coming to the United States
    d.   people who choose not to leave their homeland

Name_____ Section _____ Date _____ Score (number correct) _____ x 10 = _____

Objective: To use transitions correctly and to identify patterns of thought.

Directions: Read the following paragraphs from a college social science textbook. Fill in the blanks in each paragraph with the appropriate transition words or phrases. Then answer the questions following the paragraph.

_____1. [1]On a worldwide basis, death rates are highest in tropical Africa. [2]_____ urban, industrial nations have low death rates as well as low birthrates.
    a. As
    b. On the other hand
    c. Illustrate
    d. Compare

_____2. [3]However, some less urban and industrial nations, such as Thailand, Turkey, and Ecuador, also exhibit low death rates, _____ their birthrates are moderate or high.
    a. different from
    b. leading to
    c. even though
    d. for example

_____3. [4]The _____ for this disparity is that the percentage of young people is higher in developing countries than it is in developed countries. Still, in 2009 the death rate in the United States was 8.38 per 1,000, whereas in Sierra Leone it was 20.62 per 1,000.

—Adapted from Perry and Perry, *Contemporary Society: An Introduction to Social Science,* 13th ed., p. 263.

    a. reason
    b. result
    c. effect
    d. including

_____4. The relationship between sentence 1 and sentence 2 is _____.
    a. cause and effect
    b. generalization and example
    c. contrast
    d. definition

_____5. The relationship of sentence 4 to sentence 3 is _____.
    a. cause and effect
    b. definition and example
    c. comparison and contrast
    d. generalization and example

117

_____6. [1]Death can result from a number of _____: for instance, traffic accidents, suicide, disease, or starvation.
      a. in contrast
      b. causes
      c. examples
      d. than

_____7. [3]The great leveler of death rates has been Western medical technology, which has reached almost every corner of the world. [4]Western medical technology is the _____ for the dramatically decreased death rates everywhere.
      a. example
      b. contrast
      c. reason
      d. leads to

_____8. [5]Decreasing death rates, in fact, are a major _____ of excessive population growth in Third World nations.

—Adapted from Perry and Perry, *Contemporary Society: An Introduction to Social Science*, 13th ed., p. 263.

      a. instance
      b. meaning
      c. cause
      d. contrast

_____9. The relationship between the parts of the first sentence is _____.
      a. cause and effect
      b. example
      c. comparison
      d. contrast

_____10. The relationship between sentence 3 and sentence 4 is _____.
      a. cause and effect
      b. generalization and example
      c. comparison
      d. contrast

Name_____ Section _____ Date _____ Score (number correct) _____ x 10 = _____

Directions: Read each of the following sentences and identify the pattern of thought as indicated by the transitions.

_____1. Compulsive gambling is an example of a mental disorder.
  a. generalization and example
  b. comparison
  c. cause and effect
  d. definition and example

_____2. Effective communication skills lead to healthier relationships.
  a. cause and effect
  b. comparison
  c. generalization and example
  d. contrast

_____3. Listening and hearing differ in significant ways.
  a. definition and example
  b. contrast
  c. cause and effect
  d. comparison

Directions: Read the following paragraph and answer the questions that follow.

[1]Both President Ford and President Carter were men of decency and integrity, but neither earned a reputation as a strong, dynamic leader. [2]Although many Americans admired each man's honesty and sincerity, neither had the full confidence of the American people. [3]Moreover, neither leader had a clear sense of direction. [4]Both Ford and Carter seemed to waffle on major issues of public policy. [5]As a result, both became thought of as unsure, indecisive presidents. [6]For example, Ford began his term by urging tax increases, but later he called for a large tax cut. [7]Similarly, early on, Carter spoke of cutting military spending. [8]However, by the end of his term, he had come to support the idea of increasing defense spending.

—Adapted from Martin et al., *America and Its Peoples:
A Mosaic in the Making,* 3rd ed., pp. 1087–1088.

_____4. The phrase *but neither* in sentence 1 signals _____
  a. definition
  b. comparison
  c. contrast
  d. cause and effect

119

_____5. The phrase *although* in sentence 2 signals _____
      a. definition
      b. comparison
      c. contrast
      d. cause and effect

_____6. The transition *both* in sentence 4 signals _____.
      a. definition
      b. comparison
      c. contrast
      d. cause and effect

_____7. The transition *as a result* in sentence 5 signals _____.
      a. definition
      b. comparison
      c. contrast
      d. cause and effect

_____8. The relationship between sentence 6 and sentence 7 is _____.
      a. definition
      b. comparison
      c. contrast
      d. cause and effect

_____9. The relationship between sentence 7 and sentence 8 is _____.
      a. definition
      b. comparison
      c. contrast
      d. cause and effect

_____10. The primary pattern of thought in this paragraph is _____.
      a. definition
      b. comparison and contrast
      c. generalization and example
      d. cause and effect

Name_____ Section _____ Date _____ Score (number correct) _____ x 10 = _____

Directions: Read each of the following sentences and identify the pattern of thought as indicated by the transitions.

_____1. PepsiCo is an example of a conglomerate, a giant corporation composed of many smaller corporations.
    a. generalization and example
    b. comparison
    c. cause and effect
    d. definition and example

_____2. The consequences of failing to read assignments before a class will be poor quiz grades.
    a. cause and effect
    b. comparison
    c. generalization and example
    d. contrast

_____3. Psychologists and psychiatrists differ in the nature and amount of education they have.
    a. definition and example
    b. contrast
    c. cause and effect
    d. comparison

Directions: Read the paragraphs below and answer the questions that follow.

The means by which a communication is presented—its medium—influences people's receptiveness to attitude change. Today, one of the most common avenues for attempts at attitude change is the mass media, particularly television. After all, the goal of TV commercials is either to change or to reinforce people's behavior. Commercials exhort viewers to drink Pepsi instead of Coke, to say no to drugs, or to vote for a Democrat *instead of* a Republican. Research shows that TV advertising is one of the most influential media for changing attitudes in the Western world; this is not too surprising, given the fact that the television is on for more than 4 hours every day in the average American household.

Nevertheless, face-to-face communication often has more impact than communication through television or in writing. Thus, even though candidates for public office rely heavily on TV, radio, and printed ads, they also try to meet people face to face, sometimes taking bus or train tours to deliver their message directly to the people.

—Lefton & Brannon, *Psychology,* 8th ed., pp. 445–446.

_____4. A key word in the first sentence of this paragraph that signals a cause-and-effect pattern is _____.
    a. communication
    b. medium
    c. people's
    d. influences

_____5. According to the paragraph, what has the most persuasive effect?
     a. television
     b. radio
     c. face-to-face contact
     d. a well-designed Web site

_____6. According to the first paragraph, the desired effect of TV commercials is _____.
     a. to entertain audience
     b. to provide breaks
     c. to change behavior
     d. to persuade voters

_____7. The relationship between the second and first paragraph is one of _____.
     a. definition
     b. comparison
     c. contrast
     d. cause and effect

_____8. The transition word that indicates the relationship between the second and first paragraph is

    _____.
     a. *often*
     b. *nevertheless*
     c. *thus*
     d. *also*

_____9. Of the transition words in the second paragraph, which indicates a cause-and-effect pattern in the second paragraph?
     a. *instead of*
     b. *nevertheless*
     c. *thus*
     d. *also*

_____10. The primary pattern of thought of this passage is _____.
     a. definition
     b. comparison and contrast
     c. generalization and example
     d. cause and effect

Name_____ Section _____ Date _____Score (number correct) _____ x 10 = _____

Objective: To use transitions correctly and to identify patterns of thought.

A. Directions: Read each of the following sentences and identify the pattern of thought.

_____1. Similarly, students who binge drink were more likely than other students to report exposure to harmful drugs.
a. generalization and example
b. comparison
c. cause and effect
d. definition and example

_____2. Nicotine is a powerful central nervous system stimulant that produces a variety of physiological effects.
a. cause and effect
b. comparison
c. generalization and example
d. contrast

_____3. Made in India or southeast Asia, bidis, however, are far more toxic than cigarettes.
a. cause and effect
b. comparison
c. generalization and example
d. contrast

B. Directions: Read the following paragraphs and answer the questions that follow.

[1]Human behavior is too complex for sociologists to predict any individual's actions precisely. [2]Astronomers calculate the movement of objects in the skies with remarkable precision, but comets and planets are nonthinking objects. [3]Humans, in contrast, have minds of their own. [4]For example, no two people react to any event, whether it be a sports victory or a natural disaster, in exactly the same way.

—Adapted from Macionis, *Sociology*, 14th ed., p. 33.

_____4. The first sentence is contains a(n) _____.
a. example
b. comparison
c. generalization
d. cause and effect

_____5. The relationship between the parts of sentence 2 is one of _____.
a. cause and effect
b. comparison
c. generalization and example
d. contrast

_____6. The relationship between sentences 2 and 3 is one of _____.
  a. cause and effect
  b. comparison
  c. generalization and example
  d. contrast

_____7. The primary pattern of thought in this paragraph is _____.
  a. definition and example
  b. comparison and contrast
  c. generalization and example
  d. cause and effect

C. Directions: Read the following paragraphs and answer the questions that follow.

[1]**Conservation biology** is a scientific discipline devoted to understanding the factors, forces, and processes that influence the loss, protection, and restoration of biological diversity. [2]For instance, conservation biologists aim to develop solutions to such problems as habitat degradation and species loss. [3]They integrate an understanding of evolution and extinction with ecology and the dynamic nature of environmental systems. [4]They use field data, lab data, theory, and experiments to study our impacts on other organisms. [5]They also design, test, and implement ways to alleviate human impact.

—Adapted from Withgott and Laposata, *Essential Environment: The Science Behind the Stories,* 4th ed., p. 174.

_____8. The transition *for instance* in sentence 2 signals that _____ will follow.
  a. examples
  b. comparisons
  c. contrasts
  d. causes and effects

_____9. The purpose of sentences 3, 4, and 5 is to provide _____ for the main point.
  a. definitions
  b. comparisons
  c. examples
  d. causes and effects

_____10. The primary pattern of thought in this paragraph is _____.
  a. definition and example
  b. comparison and contrast
  c. generalization and example
  d. cause and effect

CHAPTER 8: MORE THOUGHT PATTERNS
Lab 8.6 MASTERY TEST 2

Name_____ Section _____ Date _____ Score (number correct) _____ x 10 = _____

Objective: To use transitions correctly and to identify patterns of thought.

A. Directions: Read each of the following sentences and identify the pattern of thought.

_____1. A hero is a person willing to give up everything for the sake of another, expecting nothing in return. Many of the nation's firefighters embody such heroism.
    a. cause and effect
    b. definition and example
    c. comparison and contrast
    d. generalization and example

_____2. Research remains unclear on the effects of media on the violent behavior of young people.
    e. cause and effect
    f. definition and example
    g. comparison and contrast
    h. generalization and example

_____3. The main character in the short story "A Rose for Emily" by William Faulkner and the main character in "The Yellow Wallpaper" by Charlotte Perkins Gilman both struggle with insanity.
    i. cause and effect
    j. definition and example
    k. comparison and contrast
    l. generalization and example

_____4. "All my friends do it" is an example of a kind of thinking called jumping on the bandwagon.
    m. cause and effect
    n. contrast
    o. comparison
    p. generalization and example

B. Directions: Read the following paragraphs and answer the questions that follow.

[1]To gain a better idea of what *social structure* is, think of college football. [2]You probably know the various positions on the team: center, guards, tackles, ends, quarterback, running backs, and the like. [3]Each is a *status;* that is, each is a social position with an expected role to attach to it. [4]The center is expected to snap the ball, the quarterback to pass it, the guards to block, and so on. [5]Those *role expectations* guide each player's actions; that is, the players try to do what their particular role requires. [6]Even if you graduate and return five years later, the game will still be played, although the players have changed.

125

[7]This scenario is very similar to *social structure*, the framework around which a group exists. [8]In this football example, that framework consists of the coaching staff and the eleven playing positions. [9]When someone leaves a position, the game can go on because someone else takes over that position or status and plays the role.

[10]Even though you may not play football, you nevertheless live your life within a clearly established social structure. [11]The statuses you occupy and the roles you play were already in place before you were born. [12]You take your particular positions in life, others do the same, and society goes about its business. [13]Although the specifics change with time, the game—whether of life or of football—goes on.

—Henslin, *Essentials of Sociology,* 5th ed., p. 85.

_____5. The transition *similar* in sentence 7 signals _____.
   a. definition
   b. comparison
   c. example
   d. cause and effect

_____6. An example of social structure is provided by _____.
   a. role expectations
   b. college graduates
   c. a college football team
   d. frameworks

_____7. The relationship of sentence 8 to sentence 7 is one of _____.
   a. comparison
   b. contrast
   c. example
   d. cause and effect

_____8. The transition *because* in sentence 9 signals that _____ will follow.
   a. definition
   b. comparison
   c. contrast
   d. causes and effect

_____9. The transition *although* in sentence 13 signals _____.
   a. definition
   b. contrast
   c. example
   d. cause and effect

_____10. The primary pattern of thought in this paragraph is _____.
   a. definition and example
   b. comparison and contrast
   c. generalization and example
   d. cause and effect

Name_____ Section _____ Date _____ Score (number correct) _____ x 10 = _____

Objective: To identify an author's use of facts and opinions in reading passages.

Directions: Read the statements and decide if they are facts, opinions, or a combination of fact and opinion.

_____1. Upon entering college, freshmen must take an English proficiency test to determine their readiness for college-level writing.
    a. fact
    b. opinion
    c. combination of fact and opinion

_____2. The horrific noise from the vuvuzela horns was extremely annoying to those watching the World Cup soccer games on television.
    a. fact
    b. opinion
    c. combination of fact and opinion

_____3. The Deepwater Horizon Oil Spill (caused by a drilling rig explosion in April 2010 in the Gulf of Mexico) is the largest offshore oil spill in U.S. history.
    a. fact
    b. opinion
    c. combination of fact and opinion

_____4. Michael Jackson, undisputed king of pop, is recognized as the most successful entertainer of all time by Guinness World Records.
    a. fact
    b. opinion
    c. combination of fact and opinion

_____5. Twilight is a series of four vampire-based fantasy romance novels that has everyone swooning over its brooding characters.
    a. fact
    b. opinion
    c. combination of fact and opinion

_____6. Proponents of the acai berry diet spout ridiculous claims and unsupported hype concerning its potential for miraculous weight-loss.
    a. fact
    b. opinion
    c. combination of fact and opinion

Directions: Read the following paragraph and answer the questions that follow.

[1]When you think of today's "hottest brands," what names come to mind? Coca-Cola? Nike? Google? [2]But scan last year's list of hottest brands, prepared by respected brand consultancy Landor Associates, and you'll find an unlikely entry—Las Vegas. [3]Most people wouldn't even think of Vegas as a "product," let alone as a brand. [4]But there it is, number two on the list of the nation's hottest brands, right behind Google. [5]Many old-timers still think of Las Vegas as "Sin City"—an anything-goes gambling town. [6]Vegas was built on smoke-filled casinos, bawdy all-girl revues, all-you-can-eat buffets, Elvis impersonators, and no-wait weddings. [7]But that's the old Las Vegas. [8]The new Vegas has reinvented itself as a luxury destination. [9]Casinos and gaming now account for less than half of the city's revenues. [10]Instead, the new Las Vegas brims with classy resorts, expensive shopping malls, and gourmet restaurants.

—Adapted from Kotler and Armstrong, *Principles of Marketing*, 13th ed., p. 222.

_____7. Sentence 2 is an example of _____.
   a. fact
   b. opinion
   c. combination of fact and opinion

_____8. A biased word in sentence 2 is _____.
   a. *brands*
   b. *unlikely*
   c. *consultancy*
   d. *entry*

_____9. Sentence 3 is an example of _____.
   a. fact
   b. opinion
   c. combination of fact and opinion

_____10. A biased word in sentence 10 is _____.
   a. *instead*
   b. *resorts*
   c. *new*
   d. *classy*

Name_____ Section _____ Date _____ Score (number correct) _____ x 10 = _____

Objective: To identify an author's use of facts and opinions in reading passages.

A. Directions: Read the following statements adapted from Withgott and Laposata's text, *Essential Environment: The Science Behind the Stories*, 4th ed., p. 388, and decide if they are facts, opinions, or a combination of fact and opinion.

_____1. Landfills are foul-smelling eyesores, health threats, and civic blemishes.
    a. fact
    b. opinion
    c. combination of fact and opinion

_____2. By documenting what actually happens to trash and to recyclables, researchers from MIT hope to help make the trash removal process more effective and to encourage better recycling.
    a. fact
    b. opinion
    c. combination of fact and opinion

_____3. They are affixing tiny sensors to everyday items in our trash and monitoring them to reveal their travels.
    a. fact
    b. opinion
    c. combination of fact and opinion

_____4. The results from Seattle reveal some expected patterns but also some odd surprises.
    a. fact
    b. opinion
    c. combination of fact and opinion

_____5. The longest-traveling piece of trash was a cell phone that was transported over 3,000 miles to the other corner of the United States, ending up near Ocala, Florida.
    a. fact
    b. opinion
    c. combination of fact and opinion

B. Directions: Read the following paragraph and answer the questions that follow.

[1]Time and again, Netflix has made the most profit in the distribution of video entertainment. [2]In the early 2000s, Netflix's revolutionary DVD-by-mail service put all but the most powerful movie-rental stores out of business. [3]In 2007, Netflix moved into digital streaming, which gave people a new way to access movies and other video content. [4]Now, the video distribution has become a boiling, roiling pot of emerging technologies and high-tech competitors, one that offers both mind-bending opportunities and stomach-churning risks.

—Adapted from Kotler and Armstrong, *Principles of Marketing,* 15th ed., p. 338.

_____6. Sentence 1 is an example of _____.
   a. fact
   b. opinion
   c. combination of fact and opinion

_____7. A biased word in sentence 2 is _____.
   a. 2000s
   b. revolutionary
   c. but
   d. out of business

_____8. Sentence 3 is an example of _____.
   a. fact
   b. opinion
   c. combination of fact and opinion

_____9. A biased word in sentence 4 is _____.
   a. now
   b. technologies
   c. mind-bending
   d. opportunities

____10. Sentence 4 is an example of _____.
   a. fact
   b. opinion
   c. combination of fact and opinion

Name_____ Section _____ Date _____ Score (number correct) _____ x 10 = _____

A. Directions: Read the statements and decide if they are facts, opinions, or a combination of fact and opinion

_____1. The government should reduce the growth of Medicare spending.
    a.   fact
    b.   opinion
    c.   combination of fact and opinion

_____2. Many public schools do not offer information about birth control.
    a.   fact
    b.   opinion
    c.   combination of fact and opinion

_____3. Because of the Monica Lewinsky affair, President Clinton was considered one of the most immoral presidents of the 20th century.
    a.   fact
    b.   opinion
    c.   combination of fact and opinion

_____4. President Bush is the 43rd president of the United States, but there have been only 42 presidents.
    a.   fact
    b.   opinion
    c.   combination of fact and opinion

_____5. The size of the universe is mind-boggling; the sun is only one of the more than 200 billion stars in our galaxy, the Milky Way, and the Milky Way is one of billions of galaxies in the universe.
    a.   fact
    b.   opinion
    c.   combination of fact and opinion

_____6. Mecca is a city in Saudi Arabia with 618,000 inhabitants; Mecca is located about 80 kilometers from the Red Sea coast and is built around a natural well.
    a.   fact
    b.   opinion
    c.   combination of fact and opinion

B. Directions: Read the following paragraph and answer the questions that follow.

[1]College student gambling appears to be on the rise on college campuses across the nation. [2]It was reported that in 2005, 15.5 percent of college students reported gambling once a week, up from 8.3 percent in 2002, an 87 percent increase. [3]College students have easier access to gambling opportunities than ever before with the advent of online gambling. [4]Many young people are spending an unhealthy amount of time and money participating in online poker tournaments. [5]Whereas casual gamblers can stop anytime they wish and are capable of seeing the necessity to do so, compulsive gamblers are unable to control the urge to gamble, even in the face of devastating consequences: high debt, legal problems, and the loss of everything meaningful.

—Adapted from Donatelle, *Access to Health*, 10th ed., p. 355.

_____7. A biased word in sentence 1 is _____.
     a. gambling
     b. appears
     c. rise
     d. college

_____8. Sentence 2 is an example of _____.
     a. fact
     b. opinion
     c. combination of fact and opinion

_____9. Sentence 3 is an example of _____.
     a. fact
     b. opinion
     c. combination of fact and opinion

_____10. A biased word in sentence 5 is _____.
     a. gamblers
     b. unable
     c. wish
     d. devastating

Name_____ Section _____ Date _____ Score (number correct) _____ x 10 = _____

Directions: Read the following paragraph and answer the questions that follow.

[1]A pioneer work in American opera was composed in 1911 by Scott Joplin (1868–1917), famous for his innovations in ragtime. [2]Titled *Treemonisha*, it was the first major opera by an African American, and in 1911 it was snubbed by the opera establishment. [3]Joplin, already a success because of his ragtime achievements, had to publish the work himself. [4]In 1915 it was finally produced and received generally unfavorable notices.

—Janaro & Altshuler, *The Art of Being Human*, 7th ed., p. 301.

_____1. Sentence 1 is an example of _____.
   a. fact
   b. opinion
   c. combination of fact and opinion

_____2. Sentence 2 is an example of _____.
   a. fact
   b. opinion
   c. combination of fact and opinion

_____3. Sentence 3 is an example of _____.
   a. fact
   b. opinion
   c. combination of fact and opinion

_____4. Sentence 4 is an example of _____.
   a. fact
   b. opinion
   c. combination of fact and opinion

[1]Two possible reasons come to mind to explain the opera's failure. [2]One may be that the opera world, almost exclusively a white institution, resented Joplin's effort to create grand opera rather than continue producing music "appropriate" for his cultural heritage. [3]Another may be that audiences who knew and loved Joplin's music were expecting a ragtime opera, but Joplin wanted to go lightly in his use of the tempo that had served him so well. [4]Although there is some ragtime, he may have wanted to show that music transcended narrow racial ties.

—Janaro & Altshuler, *The Art of Being Human*, 7th ed., pp. 301–302.

_____5. Sentence 2 is an example of _____.
   a. fact
   b. opinion
   c. combination of fact and opinion

133

_____6. Sentence 3 is an example of _____.
   a. fact
   b. opinion
   c. combination of fact and opinion

_____7. Sentence 4 is an example of _____.
   a. fact
   b. opinion
   c. combination of fact and opinion

[1]As happens over and over in the history of humanities, time has reversed the original criticism. [2]*Treemonisha* is now widely accepted as the first truly American opera, using American subject matter and American folk themes along with a symphonic score inspired by Wagner's music. [3]Although Joplin did in fact admire Wagner above all composers and even followed in the German composer's footsteps by writing both libretto and music, the result has been a recognized masterpiece in the romantic tradition that combines traditional forms with American motifs.

_____8. Sentence 1 is an example of _____.
   a. fact
   b. opinion
   c. combination of fact and opinion

_____9. Sentence 2 is an example of _____.
   a. fact
   b. opinion
   c. combination of fact and opinion

_____10. Sentence 3 is an example of _____.
   a. fact
   b. opinion
   c. combination of fact and opinion

Name_____ Section _____ Date _____ Score (number correct) _____ x 10 = _____

A. Directions: Read the following paragraph and decide if the statements are fact, opinion, or a combination of both.

[1]These two cities are very different: Baltimore is an Atlantic port city on Chesapeake Bay with a long history, whereas Phoenix is a young, fast-growing southwestern metropolis sprawling across the desert. [2]Each was picked by the U.S. National Science Foundation to serve as an ecological research site. [3]Since 1997, hundreds of researchers have studied Baltimore and Phoenix explicitly as ecosystems, examining nutrient cycling, biodiversity, air and water quality, how people react to environmental health threats, and more. [4]Research teams in both cities are combining old maps, aerial photos, and new remote sensing satellite data to reconstruct the history of landscape change. [5]Studies on urban ecology like these in Phoenix and Baltimore will be of vital importance in our ever more urban world.

—Adapted from Withgott and Laposata, *Essential Environment: The Science Behind the Stories*, 4th ed., p. 410.

_____1. Sentence 1 is an example of _____.
    a. fact
    b. opinion
    c. combination of fact and opinion

_____2. Sentence 2 is an example of _____.
    a. fact
    b. opinion
    c. combination of fact and opinion

_____3. Sentence 3 is an example of _____.
    a. fact
    b. opinion
    c. combination of fact and opinion

_____4. Sentence 4 is an example of _____.
    a. fact
    b. opinion
    c. combination of fact and opinion

_____5. Sentence 5 is an example of _____.
    a. fact
    b. opinion
    c. combination of fact and opinion

B. Directions: Read the following paragraph and decide if the statements are fact, opinion, or a combination of both.

[1]The circle is an archetype that affects our lives profoundly. [2]Because the circle is an unbroken line without beginning or end that encloses a uniform space, people have used it to symbolize oneness, completeness, and eternity. [3]Countless circular structures are found throughout the world: temples, stone circles, and of course, that most intriguing of all ancient monuments, Stonehenge. [4]A group of scientists waited all night on the eve of the summer solstice and were delighted when the sun's rays shone directly through the front portal. [5]Obiously, Stonehenge proves the myth that the universe is a finite circle.

—Adapted from Janaro and Altshuler, *The Art of Being Human: The Humanities as a Technique for Living*, 10th ed., p. 45.

_____ 6. Sentence 1 is an example of _____.
   a. fact
   b. opinion
   c. combination of fact and opinion

_____ 7. Sentence 2 is an example of _____.
   a. fact
   b. opinion
   c. combination of fact and opinion

_____ 8. A biased word in sentence 3 is _____.
   a. circular
   b. temples
   c. ancient
   d. intriguing

_____ 9. Sentence 4 is an example of _____.
   a. fact
   b. opinion
   c. combination of fact and opinion

_____ 10. Sentence 5 is an example of _____.
   a. fact
   b. opinion
   c. combination of fact and opinion

Name_____ Section _____ Date _____ Score (number correct) _____ x 10 = _____

Objective: To identify an author's use of facts and opinions in reading passages.

A. Directions: Read the statements and decide if they are facts, opinions, or a combination of fact and opinion.

_____1. The novel *Huckleberry Finn* by Mark Twain should be banned from required reading lists in public schools.
    a. fact
    b. opinion
    c. combination of fact and opinion

_____2. Chiropractors believe that if our spines are healthy, we will feel better and enjoy life more.
    a. fact
    b. opinion
    c. combination of fact and opinion

_____3. Many of the first modern chiropractors were jailed for practicing medicine without a license.
    a. fact
    b. opinion
    c. combination of fact and opinion

_____4. In 1944, the G.I. Bill paid for veterans to study chiropractic after they left the service.
    a. fact
    b. opinion
    c. combination of fact and opinion

_____5. A loving husband should know what his wife's emotional needs are without being told.
    a. fact
    b. opinion
    c. combination of fact and opinion

_____6. Drug use among adolescents has decreased during the past five years.
    a. fact
    b. opinion
    c. combination of fact and opinion

B. Directions: Read the following paragraph and answer the questions that follow.

[1]On April 18, 1946, the sports world focused on a baseball field in Jersey City, New Jersey, an industrial wasteland on the banks of the Passaic River. [2]It was the opening day for the Jersey City Giants of the International League. [3]Their opponents were the Montreal Royals. [4]Playing second base for the Royals was Jackie Roosevelt Robinson. [5]He was a pigeon-toed, highly competitive, marvelously talented African American athlete. [6]The stadium was filled with curious, excited spectators, and in the press box, sportswriters from all over fidgeted with their typewriters. [7]It was not just another season-opening game. [8]Professional baseball, America's national game, was about to be integrated.

—Martin et al., *America and Its People: A Mosaic in the Making,* 3rd ed., p. 948.

_____7. Sentence 1 is an example of _____.
   a. fact
   b. opinion
   c. combination of fact and opinion

_____8. A biased word in sentence 1 is _____.
   a. sports world
   b. baseball
   c. industrial
   d. wasteland

_____9. Sentence 4 is an example of _____.
   a. fact
   b. opinion
   c. combination of fact and opinion

_____10. A biased word in sentence 5 is _____.
   a. pigeon-toed
   b. marvelously
   c. African American
   d. athlete

138

Name_____ Section _____ Date _____ Score (number correct) _____ x 10 = _____

Objective: To identify the author's tone and purpose.
Directions: Choose the word that best expresses the writer's tone in the passage.

Alonzo winked at his mother's shocked gaze and with a grin quipped, "Sausage and pepperoni pizza for breakfast makes perfect sense. Allow me to demonstrate. You have your tomato. Tomato is technically a fruit. You have your cheese. Cheese is a dairy product. You have your crust—necessary carbs for quick energy in the morning. And don't forget the sausage and pepperoni—my protein. If you think about it, it's just like bacon and eggs, toast, and orange juice." Still grinning, he added, "Really it is. Well, almost. Why are you looking at me that way?"

_____1. The primary purpose of this passage is _____.
    a. to entertain
    b. to inform
    c. to persuade

_____2. The tone of this passage is _____.
    a. humorous
    b. ironic
    c. sad
    d. factual

Do you want to add years to your life and feel better too? Here are a few tips. First, to decrease your chances of a heart attack, eat a handful of nuts each day. Also, to ease the effects of rheumatoid arthritis, be sure to include some citrus, such as orange juice, in your diet. Finally, exercise on a regular basis. Include weight-bearing activities such as walking and jogging. Also, try yoga for flexibility and stress relief.

_____3. The primary purpose of this passage is _____.
    a. to entertain
    b. to inform
    c. to persuade

_____4. The tone of this passage is _____.
    a. insulting
    b. encouraging
    c. demanding
    d. exasperated

Circadian rhythms have fascinated scientists for many years. Recognizing that the eye nerves translate information to the brain about the time of day, scientists observe that we adapt to the conditions around us. Also, these researchers have recently discovered that not everyone is alike. For example, teenagers are nocturnal. That is, they are more active at night but do not function as well early in the morning.

_____5. The primary purpose of this passage is _____.
     a.   to entertain
     b.   to inform
     c.   to persuade

_____6. The tone of this passage is _____.
     a.   approving
     b.   demanding
     c.   sarcastic
     d.   objective

Because researchers studying circadian rhythms have discovered that most teenagers are really nocturnal, school administrators should take this into account when organizing a school day. For example, traditionally teenagers must arise in the predawn hours and arrive at school before sunrise. Groggy and unfocused, they find it difficult to concentrate and be alert before lunch. After lunch, which for many students in overcrowded high schools begins at 10:30 a.m., they are finally able to pay attention. Armed with this information, the school board should be innovative and rearrange the schedule, which would curb truancy in grades 8 through 12.

_____7. The primary purpose of this passage is _____.
     a.   to entertain
     b.   to inform
     c.   to persuade

_____8. The tone of this passage is _____.
     a.   informative
     b.   cynical
     c.   bossy
     d.   outraged

One of the creators of Cranium, Richard Tait, a former Microsoft executive, said he wanted to invent a game that allowed people to leave the board feeling good. He wanted a game that involved chance as well as skill, one in which people could have fun together and not feel so competitive. Four people or several teams can play one of today's hottest-selling games, Cranium. While some moves on the game board may require that a team member know the name of the largest mammal on earth (the blue whale), other moves may ask participants to hum songs, pantomime people, or spell words backward. At the end, though, all the teams feel good because they have had so much fun. Every household should purchase Cranium. You will discover it is better than TV. Also, it will stimulate your brain and encourage people to have fun together.

_____9. The primary purpose of this passage is _____.
     a.   to entertain
     b.   to inform
     c.   to persuade

_____10. The tone of this passage is _____.
     a.   accusing
     b.   positive
     c.   amused
     d.   argumentative

Name_____ Section _____ Date _____ Score (number correct) _____ x 10 = _____

Objective: To identify the author's tone and purpose.

Directions: Read the paragraphs and answer the questions that follow.

Total global fisheries catch, after decades of increases, leveled off after about 1988 and has remained fairly constant since then. This seeming stability in catch can be explained by several factors that conceal population declines: Fishing fleets are exploiting increasingly remote fishing areas, are engaging in more intensive fishing, are capturing smaller fish than before, and are targeting less desirable fish species they formerly overlooked.

—Adapted from Withgott and Laposata, *Essential Environment: The Science Behind the Stories*, 4th ed., p. 273.

_____1. The tone of this paragraph can be described as _____.
    a. objective
    b. lighthearted
    c. admiring
    d. critical

_____2. The primary purpose of this paragraph is to _____.
    a. persuade
    b. entertain
    c. inform

In the corporate world of today, where workers may become aware of defective auto parts, unsanitary food preparation, or the advertising of products they know carry a health risk, cases of selfless whistle-blowing exist. There are no easy moral victories here. If nothing else, we learn from them that doing the right thing takes not only courage but the willingness to stand quite alone. Hopefully, if you find yourself in such a situation, you too will make the right decision.

—Adapted from Janaro and Altshuler, *The Art of Being Human: The Humanities as a Technique for Living*, 10th ed., p. 368.

_____3. According to the passage, the tone could be described as _____.
    a. matter-of-fact
    b. amused
    c. playful
    d. confused

_____4. The primary purpose of this paragraph is to _____.
    a. persuade
    b. entertain
    c. inform

_____5. The underlined words indicate a tone of _____
   a. sentimentality
   b. irreverence
   c. scolding
   d. admiration

_____6. The primary purpose of this paragraph is to _____.
   a. persuade
   b. entertain
   c. inform

Just before President John F. Kennedy sent the first American troops to Vietnam in 1961, he confided to an aide: "The troops will march in; the bands will play; the crowds will cheer. . . Then we will be told we have to send more troops. It's like taking a drink. The effect wears off, and you have to take another."

—Adapted from Carnes and Garraty, *The American Nation: A History of the United States,* 14th ed., p. 765.

_____7. The tone of this passage is _____.
   a. calm
   b. cheerful
   c. gloomy
   d. encouraging

_____8. The primary purpose of this paragraph is to _____.
   a. persuade
   b. entertain
   c. inform

Millennials (people born between 1980 and 2000) withdraw to the privacy of their rooms in order to socialize. For their part, most Millennials think the Internet has improved social relations. "I've outsourced my social life exclusively to Facebook," one Millennial explained in 2009. "My time on Facebook substitutes for face time and has made my life more organized and efficient."

—Adapted from Carnes and Garraty, *The American Nation: A History of the United States,* 14th ed., p. 843.

_____9. The tone of this passage is _____.
   a. demanding
   b. approving
   c. ironic
   d. insulting

_____10. The primary purpose of this paragraph is to _____.
   a. persuade
   b. entertain
   c. inform

Name_____ Section _____ Date _____ Score (number correct) _____ x 10 = _____

A. Directions: Read the paragraphs and answer the questions that follow.

Racial prejudice is a sin against humanity. How does one dare to think less of another human being simply because of color or ethnic origin? How does one dare to think of oneself as so much more special or righteous than another? To do so is the height of arrogance. And those who sit in silence as discrimination takes place are no better than those who discriminate. Those who sit in silence and listen to words of hate are no better than those who speak those very words. Shame on those whose love of their own color drives them to hate those of different hues. Shame on those whose love of their own voices drowns out the rich tones of diversity. Shame on those of us who let them.

_____1. The primary purpose of this paragraph is _____.
   a. to entertain
   b. to inform
   c. to persuade

_____2. The tone of this passage is _____.
   a. flattering
   b. approving
   c. sarcastic
   d. outraged

While few equate immorality with criminality, the similarities are striking. First, moral codes and laws are linguistically expressed, often employing words such as *shall* and *shall not.* Second, at the heart of both concepts is the idea of intentionality, meaning that it is reasonable to hold people both morally and legally responsible for behavior that they intended to happen. Third, most believe that it is appropriate to punish people who violate both moral codes and criminal statutes, unless those people happen to be very young. Finally, there is considerable overlap between the acts that are considered criminal [and those considered immoral].

—Ellis & Walsh, *Criminology,* pp. 313–14.

_____3. The tone of this paragraph can be described as _____.
   a. emotional
   b. neutral
   c. disbelieving
   d. ironic

_____4. The primary purpose of this paragraph is to _____.
   a. persuade
   b. entertain
   c. inform

Renewed

The afternoon finds me, on the front porch in the same rocker
mother used to quiet our baby fears, searching for peace.
The steady plop of rain drops on the mulch in the azalea beds,
the fresh, sweet scent of the newly washed earth,
the glistening greens of grass, and trees, and shrubs,
the steamy mist rising from the black top road,
All awaken me to a moment created by Hands
stronger and more sure than mine.
And peace comes to me.

—Unknown

_____ 5. The purpose of this poem is _____.
     a. to entertain the reader with personal thoughts about the soothing effects of nature
     b. to persuade the reader to protect the environment
     c. to inform the reader about facts related to nature

B. Directions: Read this passage and answer the questions that follow.

How Relationships End

[1]A declining relationship usually follows one of several paths. [2]Sometimes a relationship loses steam and runs down like a dying battery. Instead of a single event that causes the breakup, the relationship **fades away**—the two partners just drift further and further apart. [3]They spend less time together, let more time go by before seeing each other again. [4]You've probably had a number of friendships that ended this way—perhaps long-distance relationships. [5]Long-distance relationships require a great deal of effort to maintain, so a move can easily decrease the level of intimacy.

[6]Some relationships end in sudden death. [7]As the name suggests, **sudden death** moves straight to separation. [8]One partner might move away or die, or more frequently, a single event such as infidelity, breaking a confidence, a major conflict, or some other major violation precipitates the breakup. [9]Sudden death is like taking an express elevator from a top floor to ground level.

[10]In between fading away and sudden death lies incrementalism. [11]**Incrementalism** is the process by which conflicts and problems continue to accumulate in the relationship until they reach a critical mass that leads to the breakup; the relationship becomes intolerable or, from a social exchange perspective, too costly. [12]"I just got to a point where it wasn't worth it anymore," and "It got to the point where all we did was fight all the time," are typical statements about incremental endings.

—Beebe, Beebe, & Redmond, _Interpersonal Communication_, 3rd ed., pp. 344–45.

_____ 6. The topic of the passage is _____.
     a. the sudden death of a relationship
     b. the paths declining relationships take as they end
     c. incrementalism
     d. what makes a good relationship

_____7. The central idea of the passage is expressed in which sentence?
      a. sentence 1
      b. sentence 2
      c. sentence 6
      d. sentence 11

_____8. The word *perspective* as it is used in sentence 11 means _____.
      a. discussion
      b. view
      c. exchange
      d. translation

_____9. The purpose of this passage is
      a. to inform the reader of the paths declining relationships take.
      b. to persuade the reader not to get entangled in a new relationship.
      c. to entertain the reader with relationship failure stories.
      d. to persuade the reader of ways to avoid a declining relationship.

_____10. "I just got to a point where it wasn't worth it anymore" and "It got to the point where all we did was fight all the time." What is the tone of these comments from paragraph 3?
      a. bias
      b. relief
      c. joy
      d. exasperation

Name_____ Section _____ Date _____ Score (number correct) _____ x 10 = _____

Directions: Choose the word that best expresses the writer's tone in the passage.

In naval aviation, the AWACS (Airborne Early Warning Command and Control System) plane, or Hawkeye, serves as an air traffic controller, monitoring the airspace around a carrier fleet. It is responsible for surveillance of enemy aircraft and ships as well as directing helicopters to survivors and guarding against air collisions. In addition to servicing the Navy, Hawkeye planes have been used in rescue operations of civilians during hurricane evacuations.

_____1. The primary purpose of this passage is _____.
    a. to entertain
    b. to inform
    c. to persuade

_____2. The tone of this passage is _____.
    a. humorous
    b. ironic
    c. confident
    d. factual

The pilots of the Hawkeye aircraft are the unsung heroes of naval operations. The first in and the last out, these men receive none of the glory bestowed on the Top Guns of F-18 fame. Thanks to Hollywood, fighter pilots have been glorified, but the pilots of the AWACS planes work quietly and diligently, and they deserve praise for their contributions.

_____3. The primary purpose of this passage is _____.
    a. to entertain
    b. to inform
    c. to persuade

_____4. The tone of this passage is _____.
    a. admiring
    b. ironic
    c. unbiased
    d. humorous

Tobacco companies have been in litigation, facing charges that their marketing practices in the past have targeted teenagers. Also, evidence indicates that companies adjusted levels of nicotine in their cigarettes to increase the probability that smokers would become addicted to the product to ensure higher sales in the future.

_____5. The primary purpose of this passage is _____.
    a. to entertain
    b. to inform
    c. to persuade

_____6. The tone of this passage is _____.

      a.   horrified

      b.   bitter

      c.   regretful

      (d.) objective

Tobacco companies should be forced to pay lucrative settlements to anyone who has become addicted or adversely affected by the use of their products. Anyone who has a loved one who has succumbed to the temptation to use cigarettes can attest to the way the product can swallow souls as well as consumers' wallets. The clinical evidence of the devastation created by secondhand smoke is compelling enough for legislators to consider legal action against the powerful corporations. Unfortunately, tobacco companies have traditionally provided strong financial support for many political candidates. Write your congressional representative and express your outrage!

_____7. The primary purpose of this passage is _____.

      a.   to entertain

      b.   to inform

      (c.) to persuade

_____8. The tone of this passage is _____.

      (a.) outraged

      b.   sad

      c.   surprised

      d.   confused

Game night at our house was hilarious when we played Cranium with two teams of three. Imagine Abram, the savvy surfer, doing an impression of Marilyn Monroe singing "Happy Birthday." Or Dave, the macho bodybuilder, swinging his hips and singing a medley of Madonna's songs. But the most memorable was George's Cranium Doodle hint for the architectural term "flying buttress." It was, well, side-splittingly outrageous!

_____9. The primary purpose of this passage is _____.

      (a.) to entertain

      b.   to inform

      c.   to persuade

_____10. The tone of this passage is _____.

      a.   accusing

      (b.) lively

      c.   critical

      d.   argumentative

Name_____ Section _____ Date _____ Score (number correct) _____ x 10 = _____

A. Directions: Read the paragraphs and answer the questions that follow.

The franchise organization is the most common type of contractual relationship. In this system, a channel member called a franchisor links several stages in the production-distribution process. In the United States alone, some 3,000 franchisors and 825,000 franchise outlets account for more than $2.1 trillion of economic output. Industry analysts estimate that a new franchise outlet opens somewhere in the United States every eight minutes and that about one out of every 12 retail business outlets is a franchised business. Almost every kind of business has been franchised—from motels and fast-food restaurants to dental centers and dating services, from wedding consultants and handyman services to fitness centers and funeral homes.

—Adapted from Kotler and Armstron, *Principles of Marketing*, 15th ed., p. 346.

_____1. The primary purpose of this paragraph is to _____.
    a. persuade
    b. entertain
    c. inform

_____2. The tone of this paragraph can be described as _____.
    a. critical
    b. regretful
    c. ironic
    d. objective

In the movie *As Good As It Gets* (1997), a struggling single mother works as a waitress to earn enough for her and her asthmatic son. A cranky older man finds himself attracted to her. He is obsessed with order and neatness, and the two make as unlikely a couple as has ever been seen in a romantic comedy. After acquiring good medical help for her son, the older man is enticed by her gratitude to propose marriage. The heroine's mother reminds her that this may be "as good as it gets," and the embrace in the final scene tells us reality demands that we take what we can get.

—Adapted from Janaro and Altshuler, *The Art of Being Human: The Humanities as a Technique for Living*, 10th ed., pp. z288-289.

_____3. The primary purpose of this paragraph is to _____.
    a. persuade
    b. entertain
    c. inform

_____4. The tone of this paragraph can be described as _____.
    a. critical
    b. demanding
    c. bittersweet
    d. objective

[1]To keep customers coming back, Stew Leonard's has created what the New York Times has dubbed the "Disneyland of Dairy Stores," complete with costumed characters, scheduled entertainment, a petting zoo, and animatronics throughout the store. [2]Stew Leonard's now serves more than 300,000 customers each week. This legion of loyal shoppers is largely a result of the store's passionate approach to customer service. [3]Rule #1: The customer is always right. [4]Rule #2: If the customer is ever wrong, reread rule #1."

—Lockard & Abrams, *Computers for Twenty-First Century Educators,* p. 287.

_____5. The tone of sentences 3 and 4 is _____.
      a. sorrowful and disappointed
      b. critical and arrogant
      c. informative and pessimistic
      d. humorous and entertaining

_____6. The primary purpose of this paragraph is to _____.
      a. inform
      b. entertain
      c. persuade

B. Directions: Read the passage and then answer the questions that follow it.

[1]Municipalities that provide tap water to their residents need to submit regular reports to the Environmental Protection Agency describing their sources, treatment methods, and contaminants. [2]In contrast, bottled water is regulated much more lightly as a "food" by the Food and Drug Administration. [3]Bottle companies do not have to inform the public or the government where their water comes from or how it is treated, and they are not required to test samples with certified laboratories or notify the FDA of any contamination problems.

[4]So, to find out what's in bottled water, scientists have had to do some detective work. [5]In 2008, research scientists sent samples of 10 major brands of bottled water to the University of Iowa's Hygienic Laboratory for analysis. [6]The lab's chemists ran a battery of tests and detected 38 chemical pollutants, including traces of heavy metals, radioactive isotopes, caffeine and pharmaceuticals from wastewater pollution, nitrate and ammonia from fertilizer, and various industrial compounds such as solvents and plasticizers. [7]Each brand contained eight contaminants on average, and two brands had levels of chemicals that exceeded legal limits in California and industry safety guidelines.

[8]Two brands showed the chemical composition of standard municipal water treatment. [9]Why is this surprising: An estimated 25-44% of "safer," bottled water is simply tap water, bottled and sold at high prices.

[10]So, think twice before loading your cart with packs of bottled water. Is it really better because it's in a bottle? Is the easy accessibility worth the cost? or the risk? We should all be writing our congressmen about this one!
      —Withgott and Laposata, *Essential Environment: The Science Behind the Stories, 4th ed.,* p. 268.

_____7. The topic of the passage is _____.
   a. why people should buy bottled water
   b. our water supply
   c. laboratory tests
   d. the safety of bottled water

_____8. The purpose of the passage is _____.
   a. to inform.
   b. to persuade.
   c. to entertain

_____9. Which word describes the tone in the first paragraph?
   a. humorous
   b. satirical
   c. alarming
   d. emotional

_____10. Which word describes the tone in sentences 8-9?
   a. jovial
   b. depressing
   c. ironic
   d. carefree

151

Name_____ Section _____ Date _____ Score (number correct) _____ x 10 = _____

Directions: Read the paragraphs and answer the questions that follow

Dr. Martin Luther King, Jr., was one of those rare men who fulfilled his destiny. There can be little doubt that he lived a life based on the principles of courage and sacrifice. There can be no argument that his courage and sacrifice have instilled those principles in others. He was a man who would not allow the limited views of the small-minded to define his world or direct his steps. He was a man who faced death unflinchingly so that others could live lives of which he could only dream. King was indeed a king among men.

_____1. The primary purpose of this paragraph is to _____.
      a. persuade
      b. entertain
      c. inform

_____2. The tone of this paragraph can be described as _____.
      a. critical
      b. regretful
      c. ironic
      d. admiring

Many people who begin exercise programs do so without proper preparation. This lack of preparation can lead to serious injuries. A few simple steps can help avoid these unnecessary injuries. Before the workout, stretch. Taking a few minutes to stretch warms up the muscles and prevents strains and tears. During the workout, drink plenty of water. A good workout causes a loss of body fluids through sweating. Staying hydrated ensures that muscles can perform properly. After the workout, stretch again. Stretching after the workout reduces muscle tension and improves circulation. In addition, stretching an already warmed-up muscle encourages greater range in mobility and flexibility.

_____3. The primary purpose of this paragraph is to _____.
      a. persuade
      b. entertain
      c. inform

_____4. The tone of this paragraph can be described as _____.
      a. critical
      b. demanding
      c. fearful
      d. objective

It is unlikely that human nature will suddenly change drastically—that we will abruptly lose our environmental manipulativeness. What we must seek instead are ways to be more accommodating with other species and with the biosphere. Those of us living in affluent, developed nations are responsible for the greatest amount of environmental degradation. Our long-term welfare and that of future generations demand that we work toward changing some of our values, learning to revere the natural processes that sustain us and reducing our orientation toward short-term personal gain. The current state of the biosphere demonstrates that we are treading precariously on uncharted ecological ground. The importance of our scientific and personal efforts cannot be overstated.

—Campbell, Reece, Taylor, and Simon, *Biology: Concepts & Connections*, 5th ed., 781.

_____5. The primary purpose of this paragraph is to _____.
    a. persuade
    b. entertain
    c. inform

_____6. The tone of this paragraph can be described as _____.
    a. serious
    b. humorous
    c. fearful
    d. disbelieving

[1]The suicide rate increases over the lifespan, from childhood to old age, but it jumps sharply at adolescence. [2]Currently, suicide is the third-leading cause of death (after motor vehicle collisions and homicides) among American youths and the second-leading cause (after motor vehicle collisions) among Canadian youths. [3]Perhaps because North American teenagers experience more stress and fewer supports than in the past, the adolescent suicide rate tripled in both the United States and Canada between the mid-1960s and the mid-1990s.

[4]Despite girls' higher rates of depression, the number of boys who kill themselves exceeds the number of girls by a ratio of 4 or 5 to 1. [5]Girls make more unsuccessful suicide attempts, using methods from which they are more likely to be revived, such as a sleeping pill overdose. [6]In contrast, boys tend to choose techniques that lead to instant death, such as firearms or hanging. [7]Gender-role expectations may be responsible; less tolerance exists for feelings of helplessness and failed efforts in males than in females. [8]Many depressed young people conclude that no one could possibly understand their intense pain, and their despair and hopelessness deepen.

[9]To prevent suicides, parents and teachers must be trained to pick up on the signals that a troubled teenager sends. [10] Schools, recreation, and religious organizations must all be equipped to provide sympathetic counselors, peer support groups, and telephone hot lines. [11]A watchful eye must be kept on vulnerable adolescents. [12]We must all do our part.

—Donatelle, *Access to Health*, 10th ed., p. 420.

_____7. The topic of the passage is _____.
    a. differences between suicide attempts between boys and girls
    b. stories of adolescent suicide attempts
    c. the dangers of gender-role expectations
    d. the increasing adolescent suicide rate

_____8. The purpose of the first two paragraphs is _____.
      a.   to inform
      b.   to persuade
      c.   to entertain

_____9. The purpose of the last paragraph is _____.
      a.   to inform
      b.   to persuade
      c.   to entertain

_____10. The overall tone of this passage is _____.
      a.   concerned
      b.   bitter
      c.   admiring
      d.   argumentative

Name_____ Section _____ Date _____ Score (number correct) _____ x 10 = _____

Objective: To use supporting details to make accurate inferences.

Directions: Read the passage below. Decide if the following statements are valid inferences that are firmly based on the information in the passage.

In 1999, the world's population surpassed 6 billion. Ninety-seven percent of each year's population growth occurs in the poorest parts of the world. Experts believe that by 2050, the world population will grow to over 9 billion. Many scientists think that overpopulation has caused a loss of large areas of forest and topsoil. Some also believe that uncontrolled population growth will lead to worldwide shortages of food and energy. For the past half century, people concerned about overpopulation have called for population control. The following statistics are based on current population:

- 300 million women want family planning but do not have information about it or the means to get it.
- 1 billion people have no access to health care.
- 1.3 billion people live in poverty.
- 840 million people don't have enough food to stay healthy.
- 85 countries do not have the ability to grow or buy enough food to feed their citizens.
- 1.5 billion people do not have access to safe drinking water.

—Adapted from Donatelle, *Health: The Basics*, 5th ed., p. 406.

_____1. The world will not be able to feed its population by 2050.
     a. valid inference
     b. not a valid inference

_____2. Poor people should not have children.
     a. valid inference
     b. not a valid inference

_____3. Poor people are more likely to have many children.
     a. valid inference
     b. not a valid inference

_____4. Many people are outraged by overpopulation.
     a. valid inference
     b. not a valid inference

_____5. Some people fear the effects of overpopulation.
     a. valid inference
     b. not a valid inference

_____6. The world is overpopulated.
      a.   valid inference
      b.   not a valid inference

_____7. Some people want to limit the number of children people have.
      a.   valid inference
      b.   not a valid inference

_____8. The statistics are likely to rise in the upcoming years.
      a.   valid inference
      b.   not a valid inference

_____9. Overpopulation is the main cause of starvation
      a.   valid inference
      b.   not a valid inference

_____10. About twenty percent of the population lives in poverty.
      a.   valid inference
      b.   not a valid inference

Name_____ Section _____ Date _____ Score (number correct) _____ x 10 = _____

Objective: To use supporting details to make accurate inferences.

Directions: Read the passage below. Decide if the following statements are valid inferences that are firmly based on the information in the passage.

For years discount retailer Target focused increasingly on the "Expect More" side of its "Expect More. Pay Less." value proposition. Its carefully cultivated "upscale-discounter" image successfully differentiated it from Walmart's more hard-nosed "lowest-price" position. However, when the economy soured, many consumers worried that Target's trendier assortments and hip marketing also meant higher prices, and Target's performance slipped. So Target shifted its balance more toward the "Pay Less" half of the slogan, making certain that its prices are in line with Walmart's and that customers know it. Although still trendy, Target's marketing now emphasizes more practical price and savings appeals. "We let too much space drift between 'Expect More' and 'Pay Less,'" says Target's chief marketing officer. Now, "we believe we've negated the price perception issues," says the executive.

—Adapted from Kotler and Armstrong, *Principles of Marketing*, 15th ed., p. 23.

_____1. Target's marketing focus on appealing to "upscale" consumers did not pay off when the economy declined.
     a. valid inference
     b. not a valid inference

_____2. People who shop at Target are generally wealthier than those who shop at Walmart.
     a. valid inference
     b. not a valid inference

_____3. Target discovered that its shoppers are just as interested in low prices as those consumers who shop at Walmart.
     a. valid inference
     b. not a valid inference

_____4. The prices of goods at Walmart and Target are within close range of each other.
     a. valid inference
     b. not a valid inference

_____5. When the economy "soured," Targets customers fled to Walmart, seeking lower prices.
     a. valid inference
     b. not a valid inference

Today's organizations pose a growing threat to personal privacy. Large organizations are necessary for today's society to operate. In some cases, organizations using or selling information about us may actually be helpful. However, cases of identity theft are on the rise, and personal privacy is on the decline.

For decades, the level of personal privacy in the United States has been declining. Early in the twentieth century, when state agencies began issuing driver's licenses, for example, they generated files for every licensed driver. Today, officials can send this information at the touch of a button not only to the police but also to all sorts of other organizations. The Internal Revenue Service and the Social Security Administration, as well as government agencies that benefit veterans, students, the unemployed, and the poor, all collect mountains of personal information.

In the past, small-town life gave people little privacy. But at least if people knew something about you, you were just as likely to know something about them. Today, unknown people "out there" can access information about each of us all the time without our learning about it. In part, the loss of privacy is a result of more and more complex computer technology. Are you aware that every e-mail you send and every Web site you visit leaves a record in one or more computers? These records can be retrieved by people you don't know as well as by employers and other public officials.

—Adapted from Macionis, *Sociology*, 14th ed., p. 161.

_____ 6. Companies that sell personal information are doing so illegally.
    a. valid inference
    b. not a valid inference

_____ 7. Organizations must have an individual's approval before selling his or her personal information.
    a. valid inference
    b. not a valid inference

_____ 8. Much of the loss of our personal privacy is related to our society's more advanced technology.
    a. valid inference
    b. not a valid inference

_____ 9. Your employer has the right to access email messages that you send while using company computers.
    a. valid inference
    b. not a valid inference

_____ 10. No one would be interested in keeping track of Web sites that you visit while shopping or browsing the Internet.
    a. valid inference
    b. not a valid inference

Name_____ Section _____ Date _____ Score (number correct) _____ x 10 = _____

A. Directions: Read the passage below. Decide if the following statements are valid inferences that are firmly based on the information in the passage.

Mara and Kimberly walked out to the parking lot at the same time. Each woman lugged identical sets of thick, heavy textbooks. Mara also struggled to hold on to the heavy jacket she had worn that morning. As Kimberly watched Mara battle with her coat and books, she was grateful she had grabbed only a sweater, which was now tied around her waist.

_____1. Mara and Kimberly are friends.
    a. valid inference
    b. not a valid inference

_____2. The weather warmed up during the day.
    a. valid inference
    b. not a valid inference

_____3. Mara and Kimberly take some of the same courses.
    a. valid inference
    b. not a valid inference

_____4. It is the summer season.
    a. valid inference
    b. not a valid inference

B. Directions: Read each of the following groups of sentences, and then select the letter of the accurate inference based on the details presented.

- All public restrooms in the town have the water faucets turned off and have hand sanitizers by the sink instead.
- In local public restaurants, food is served on paper plates and menus have handwritten notes, "Water will be served only on request."
- In local hotels, water fountains, which are turned off, have been replaced by containers of bottled water.

_____5. What can you infer from these details?
    a. The town is on water restrictions.
    b. The town's water supply has been contaminated.
    c. The local merchants are trying to save money by using less water.
    d. The cost of water has increased significantly in the area.

- The cottage deck railing is decorated with strings of colorful lights.
- Reggae music fills the air, and laughter ripples from the people inside, who are holding full Margarita glasses.
- The aroma of grilled blackened tuna wafts from the deck.

_____6. What can you infer from these details?
      a. People are gathered for a birthday party.
      b. The occasion is a party after a wedding.
      c. It is Christmas at the beach.
      d. People have gathered to enjoy company, music, and food.

- The sky is pewter gray.
- The temperature has dropped rapidly and now hovers around 29 degrees.
- The humidity is 90 percent, and the barometric pressure is falling.

_____7. What can you infer from these details?
      a. It will probably snow soon.
      b. The precipitation will begin as rain and taper off in a few hours.
      c. The precipitation will begin as snow and then change to rain.
      d. A hurricane is approaching.

- Rachel has cat figurines on the shelf by her bed.
- She wears a T-shirt that says, "Love me, love my cat."
- A box of kitty litter sits in the corner of the laundry room.

_____8. What can you infer from these details?
      a. Rachel's cat has run away.
      b. Rachel is a cat lover.
      c. Rachel is obsessed with cats.
      d. Rachel loves cats but is allergic to them.

C. Directions: Read the following passage and answer the questions that follow.

Asian Americans were the fastest-growing minority group in the United States at the end of the 20th century. In 1999, there were nearly 11 million Americans of Asian or Pacific Island descent. Although they represented only 3.9 percent of the total U.S. population, they were increasing at seven times the national rate. Experts believe that by 2050, one in ten Americans will be of Asian origin.

Compared to other minorities, Asian Americans are fairly well educated and **affluent**. Three out of four Asian youths graduate from high school, compared to less than one out of two for African Americans and Latinos. Asian Americans also have the highest percentage of college graduates, and they earn more doctoral degrees than any other minority group. Many Asian Americans have entered professional fields. As a result, the average income in 1998 for Asian American families was over $4,000 higher than the national average.

      —Adapted from Divine, Breen, Fredrickson, & Williams, _The American Story_, pp. 1085–86.

_____9. The best statement of the implied central idea for the passage is _____
      a. Overall, Asian immigrants are thriving in America.
      b. Asian Americans are intelligent and hardworking.
      c. Asian Americans are the fastest-growing group of people coming into the United States.
      d. Asian families encourage their children.

_____10. What logical inference can you make from the information in this paragraph?
      a. Asian Americans are smarter than other Americans.
      b. Asian immigrants face fewer problems adjusting to life in America than other minority groups.
      c. Asian Americans value education.
      d. Asian Americans have a stronger work ethic than any other group.

Name_____ Section _____ Date _____ Score (number correct) _____ x 10 = _____

Directions: Read the passage below. Decide if the following statements are valid inferences that are firmly based on the information in the passage.

[1]On an everyday basis, all of us deal with a set of issues and events ranging from personal issues (such as job or school stress, financial needs, and family demands) to global issues (such as world hunger and world peace).

[2]Often the way we word our ideas reveals our attitudes about our own sense of power. [3]According to Stephen R. Covey, author of *The Seven Habits of Highly Effective People*, most of us have either a "proactive" or "reactive" attitude. [4]For example, a reactive student who is constantly late with assignments might say, "I wish I could be on time with my assignments, but I just can't help it; something always comes up." [5]In contrast, a proactive student thinks, "I am going to set up a schedule so that I can get my assignments completed on time."

[6]A proactive individual understands that he or she must take responsibility for his or her own actions. [7]For proactive people, circumstances do not dictate success—they themselves do. [8]Feelings do not rule behaviors, and decisions are based on values and goals. [9]A perfect example of the difference between reactive and proactive attitudes can be seen in the different ways people think of love. [10]A reactive person thinks of love primarily as a feeling. [11]Thus as the feelings of love diminish, the commitment to the relationship weakens. [12]A proactive person, by contrast, looks at love as an act of will. [13]The decision to be loyal to the commitment stays strong even if feelings diminish.

_____1. A reactive person does not take responsibility for his or her actions.
      a. valid inference
      b. not a valid inference

_____2. Proactive people are usually more successful than reactive people.
      a. valid inference
      b. not a valid inference

_____3. Reactive people are more likely to be affected by circumstances (such as the weather) than proactive people are.
      a. valid inference
      b. not a valid inference

_____4. Most people are proactive.
      a. valid inference
      b. not a valid inference

_____5. "I can" is a proactive statement.
      a. valid inference
      b. not a valid inference

_____6. Proactive people are not affected by what others think of them.
   a. valid inference
   b. not a valid inference

_____7. Events do not hurt us, but how we respond to them can.
   a. valid inference
   b. not a valid inference

_____8. Once a reactive person, always a reactive person.
   a. valid inference
   b. not a valid inference

_____9. "I choose" is a reactive statement.
   a. valid inference
   b. not a valid inference

Directions: Read the following passage from a college textbook, and determine the most logical inference.

When we watch the ways individual families interact with their infants or young children and then follow the children over time to see which ones later have high or low IQs, we can begin to get some sense of the kinds of specific family interactions that foster higher scores. At least five dimensions of family interaction or stimulation seem to make a difference. Families with higher-IQ children tend to do the following:

1. They provide an *interesting and complex physical environment* for the child, including play materials that are appropriate for the child's age and developmental level.
2. They are *emotionally responsive* to and *involved* with their child. They respond warmly and contingently to the child's behavior, smiling when the child smiles, answering the child's questions, and in myriad ways reacting to the child's cues.
3. They *talk to their child* often, using language that is descriptively rich and accurate. And when they interact with the child, they operate in what Vygotsky referred to as the *zone of proximal development,* aiming their conversation, their questions, and their assistance at a level that is just above the level the child could manage on her own, thus helping the child to master new skills.
4. They avoid *excessive restrictiveness,* punitiveness, or control, instead giving the child room to explore, even opportunities to make mistakes.
5. They *expect* their child to do well and to develop rapidly. They emphasize and press for school achievement.

—Bee, *Lifespan Development,* 2nd ed., pp. 182–183.

_____10. Which statement is a valid inference based upon the details in the passage?
   a. Effective parents rely on experts to teach their children.
   b. Effective parents would probably punish a child for a poor report card.
   c. Effective parents enrich a child's vocabulary by using descriptive and accurate language when they talk to the child.
   d. Effective parents expect their children to be seen and not heard.

Name_____ Section _____ Date _____ Score (number correct) _____ x 10 = _____

A. Directions: Read the passage below. Decide if the following statements are valid inferences that are firmly based on the information in the passage.

Religious institutions have long been the backbone of communities, and the postwar period witnessed a remarkable expansion. By 1990, membership in all churches and synagogues surpassed 148 million, an increase of 60 million during the previous four decades. In 1990 two-thirds of all Americans reported that they belonged to a church, the highest percentage by far among the major industrial nations in the West.

Since 1970, however, church attendance among persons younger than sixty has declined about 20 percent. One survey found that in 1968, 9 percent of entering college freshmen said they never attended church; by 2000, that percentage had more than doubled. By the 1970s, moreover, millions of Americans went to church by turning on the TV. "Televangelists" such as Rex Humbard, Oral Roberts, Jerry Falwell, Pat Robertson, and Jim and Tammy Bakker founded their own churches and educational institutions, supported by direct appeals to viewers. A few established their own colleges, such as Falwell's Liberty University, Oral Roberts University, and Robertson's CBN University (renamed Regent University in 1990). A number of scandals involving prominent televangelists caused disillusionment and widespread defections. On the other hand, the rapid spread of cable television greatly increased the number of available channels, enabling scores of new evangelists to reach out to viewers. Community-based ministers saw congregations shrink; thousands of churches closed their doors for good.

—Adapted from Carnes and Garraty, *The American Nation: A History of the United States, 14th ed.*, p. 842.

_____1. The number of community churches has been declining.
    a. valid inference
    b. not a valid inference

_____2. Americans are the most religious people in the world.
    a. valid inference
    b. not a valid inference

_____3. The ease of attending church "by television," probably hurts attendance at community churches.
    a. valid inference
    b. not a valid inference

_____4. Belonging to a church is becoming more and more rare.
    a. valid inference
    b. not a valid inference

_____5. The number of past scandals involving television evangelists proves that they should not be trusted.
    a. valid inference
    b. not a valid inference

B. Directions: Read the passage below. Decide if the following statements are valid inferences that are firmly based on the information in the passage.

The characteristics of the homeless have changed in recent years. Where once there were elderly alcoholics or disturbed or eccentric "bag ladies," today there are many young mothers with children and whole young families whose heads have lost jobs. Where once there were wage earners out on their luck, today there are dropouts with few skills, no experience, and few prospects for a future. The problems these new homeless exhibit are of such a nature that they initiate a never-ending cycle: They include mental instability, drug and alcohol use, unemployment, lack of education and job skills, alienation from family and friends, behavior problems, personal neglect, and disregard for personal responsibility. Many had depended on public assistance and are homeless as a result of the erosion of federal subsidies. Others became homeless when state mental hospitals began discharging inmates in the 1970s following a movement whose adherents argued that the mentally ill should not be locked up unless they broke specific laws. One report to Congress noted that single men made up 51 percent of the homeless population, families with children 30 percent, single women 17 percent, and unaccompanied minors 2 percent.

—Adapted from Perry and Perry, *Contemporary Society: An Introduction to Social Science*, 13th ed., p. 166.

_____6. At least today's society has been able to help elderly alcoholics and disturbed or eccentric "bag ladies" move into homes.
    a. valid inference
    b. not a valid inference

_____7. Today more young mothers with children are homeless than ever before.
    a. valid inference
    b. not a valid inference

_____8. The future looks grim for today's homeless who have little education or job skills.
    a. valid inference
    b. not a valid inference

C. Directions: Read the passage below and answer the questions that follow.

Although people detect their surroundings mainly by sight and sound, animals of many other species have a highly developed sense of smell, with odor-detection abilities that far exceed ours. In some cases, people have taken advantage of animal olfactory abilities to solve human problems. Consider, for example, the problem of unexploded land mines. More than 100 million of these explosive devices remain buried in countries around the world, where they were planted during past wars and forgotten. They pose a major threat to the safety of millions of mostly poor, rural people. Unfortunately, the process of removing mines is slow, expensive, and very dangerous. Animals can help; for example, dogs can smell the explosive in a land mine. Dogs, however, are heavy enough to detonate a mine.

Recently, however, a new, better, animal assistant has been drafted to help find mines. In Mozambique, home to as many as 11 million mines, rats find mines. In particular, Gambian giant pouched rats have been trained to sniff out mines and, in return for a banana or peanut reward, scratch the ground vigorously when they find a mine. The rats are very light and also work very quickly. In 1 hour, two rats can search an area that would consume 2 weeks' time for a trained human with a metal detector.

—Adapted from Audesirk and Audesirk, *Biology: Life on Earth*, 10th ed., p. 471.

_____ 9. Which statement is a valid inference based upon the details in the passage?
  a. Most of the buried land mines in countries around the world probably will not explode.
  b. Most of the land mines were buried and forgotten in cities with large populations.
  c. People in Mozambique are abusing rats by putting them at risk.
  d. Although dogs can smell explosives, using them to detect land mines is not as practical as rats, because their weight will most likely set off the mine.

_____ 10. Which statement is a valid inference based upon the details in the passage?
  a. Mozambique has probably been the scene of much war and violence.
  b. Training a rat to detect a buried land mine can be accomplished fairly quickly and easily.
  c. Rats may be able to detect land mines, but their training and care is probably much more expensive than training other animals.
  d. The world has learned its lesson and will soon abolish the use of land mines.

CHAPTER 11: INFERENCES
Lab 11.6 MASTERY TEST 2

Name_____ Section _____ Date _____ Score (number correct) _____ x 10 = _____

A. Directions: Read the passage below. Decide if the following statements are valid inferences that are firmly based on the information in the passage.

William Byrd II (1674–1744) was a successful Tidewater planter. He felt at home in both London and Virginia, the state in which he was born. In 1728, at the height of his political power, Byrd agreed to help survey a boundary in dispute between North Carolina and Virginia. During his long trip through the backcountry, Byrd kept a detailed journal. His lively record of daily events is now thought of as a classic piece of early American literature. He met many highly independent people. For example, as soon as he left the world of tobacco plantations behind, he met a self-styled **"hermit"** living in the woods. The hermit, an Englishman, seemed to prefer the freedoms of the wild to the limits set by society.

—Divine, Breen, Fredrickson, & Williams, *The American Story*, p. 105.

_____1. William Byrd lived in eighteenth-century America.
    a. valid inference
    b. not a valid inference

_____2. William Byrd's journal was a record of what he saw while on his journey.
    a. valid inference
    b. not a valid inference

_____3. One of the main crops in North Carolina and Virginia was tobacco.
    a. valid inference
    b. not a valid inference

_____4. The tobacco plantations were found in the back country.
    a. valid inference
    b. not a valid inference

_____5. The hermit was born in America.
    a. valid inference
    b. not a valid inference

B. Directions: Read each of the following groups of sentences, and then select the letter of the most accurate inference based on the details presented.

- The 20 airmen move with resolve toward their jets in the predawn hours.
- Although the jets' noses have been painted with a picture representing each pilot, the actual names of the flyers have been removed for this mission.
- On one side of the runway, tearful family members and friends are clustered, waving American flags.

____ 6. The most logical inference based upon the details in the sentences is
   a. The pilots are arriving after an absence of many months.
   b. The pilots are on a routine practice mission.
   c. The pilots are leaving for a difficult mission.
   d. The pilots are nervous about their assignment.

- People are crowded into the card section of the grocery store.
- Heart-shaped balloons are in abundance near the checkout stand.
- Red-foiled pots of tulips line shelves in the florist section of the store.

____ 7. The most logical inference based upon the details in the sentences is
   a. Christmas is approaching.
   b. Valentine's Day is near.
   c. People are looking for ways to cheer their depressed friends.
   d. The grocery store caters to wealthy patrons.

- In the bookstore coffee shop, Melissa orders herbal tea with soy milk.
- She sits down to study her selections for purchase: *OM Yoga* and *Nutrition and Edible Flowers*.
- She sports well-worn jogging shoes, sweat pants, and a T-shirt that says, "Pain is weakness leaving the body."

____ 8. The most logical inference based upon the details in the sentences is
   a. Melissa is an avid jogger.
   b. Melissa has been practicing yoga for many years.
   c. Melissa is thinking of taking up a new exercise program.
   d. Melissa has an interest in nutrition and exercise.

C. Directions: Read the passages below and answer the questions that follow.

The founder of classical criminology is the seventeenth-century Italian nobleman and professor of law Cesare Beccaria (1738–1794). Beccaria published the first book to advocate fundamentally reforming Europe's judicial and penal systems. The book, titled *Dei Delitti e della Pene* (On Crimes and Punishment), was an impassioned plea to make the criminal justice system rational in the sense that it was based on humanistic principles and an appeal to reason.

Beccaria's philosophy contrasted with many common practices in seventeenth-century Europe. For example, during the 1700s, the penalties imposed by judges were quite harsh, and punishment was a source of public entertainment. Torture was often used to extract confessions from suspects.

—Ellis & Walsh, *Criminology*, p. 83.

_____9. Which statement is a valid inference based upon the details in the passage?
    a. Cesare Beccaria was a ruthless, vengeful ruler.
    b. Cesare Beccaria sought to change the justice system because it was unfair.
    c. Cesare Beccaria sought laws that instilled justice rather than revenge. Although torture was used in other European countries, it was never used in Italy.
    d. Torture was used as a punishment only in Italy.

Russian psychologist Lev Vygotsky, who was born the same year as Piaget [1896] but died at the early age of 38, is normally thought of as belonging to the cognitive-development camp, but he placed emphasis somewhat differently. In particular, he was convinced that complex forms of thinking have their origins in *social* interactions rather than in the child's private explorations. According to Vygotsky, children's learning of new cognitive skills is guided by an adult (or a more skilled child, such as an older sibling), who models and structures the child's learning experience, a process called *scaffolding*. Such new learning, Vygotsky suggested, is best achieved in what he called the **zone of proximal development**—that range of tasks that are too hard for the child to do alone but that he can manage with guidance. As the child becomes more skilled, the zone of proximal development steadily shifts upward, including ever-harder tasks.

—Bee, *Lifespan Development,* 2nd ed., p. 37.

_____10. Which statement is a valid inference based upon the details in the passage?
    a. Sometimes parents and teachers try to teach children new skills before they are ready.
    b. Vygotsky believed that children could learn anything if they are left to explore on their own.
    c. Vygotsky felt that teachers and parents were unimportant in a child's cognitive development.
    d. Scaffolding teaches children new things by making huge leaps from one stage to another without guidance.

Name_____ Section _____ Date _____ Score (number correct) _____ x 10 = _____

Objective: To identify the claim and support in an argument.

A. Directions: Read all of the statements for each question and choose the claim.

_____1. Which one of the following sentences states the claim for this group of ideas?
   a. People who rent their homes never make money in the transaction, and they are not in control when the monthly payments are increased.
   b. Homeowners can build up equity and eventually show a profit from their investment years later.
   c. People should be encouraged to own a home rather than rent.
   d. People who own their own homes take more pride in their community.

_____2. Which one of the following sentences states the claim for this group of ideas?
   a. Athletes often develop a network that proves advantageous when they begin job hunting.
   b. Participation in sports in college enhances a student's academic and professional life.
   c. Coaches often keep a vigilant eye on their team members' grades, so the athletes often get special academic privileges such as early registration and access to excellent tutors.
   d. Many companies recruit former athletes because of their leadership and team skills.

_____3. Which one of the following sentences states the claim for this group of ideas?
   a. Reading aloud provides an opportunity for parents and young children to sit closely and enjoy some time alone, without the distractions of a TV, video game, or computer.
   b. When parents read aloud to their adolescent children, they are sending the message, "I value you, and I value your education."
   c. Reading aloud to children of all ages builds long-term bonds.
   d. Snuggling with a child during reading time helps to create a sense of security.

B. Directions: Read the paragraph and determine whether the sentences state the claim or support for an argument.

[1]Because they are plentiful and require little land or maintenance, insects are an economical food source. [2]In many countries, eating bugs is a part of the culture's cuisine. [3]Fried grubs, for example, are a tasty treat in Australia. [4]Because they are low in cholesterol, insects make a healthful meal. [5]Many third-world countries also exist on grazing animals. [6]Insects are a viable, healthful food source and should be marketed worldwide.

_____4. Sentence 1 states the _____.
   a. claim
   b. support
   c. This sentence is not relevant information.

_____5. Sentence 2 states the _____.
   a. claim
   b. support
   c. This sentence is not relevant information.

_____6. Sentence 4 states the _____.
   a. claim
   b. support
   c. This sentence is not relevant information.

_____7. Sentence 5 states the _____.
   a. claim
   b. support
   c. This sentence is not relevant information.

_____8. Sentence 6 states the _____.
   a. claim
   b. support
   c. This sentence is not relevant information.

C. Directions: Read the paragraph and answer the questions that follow.

[1]Injury is not only possible but probable. [2]In the face of this risk, the athlete's heart pounds with excitement, and the thought of turning back is overcome by the anticipation of the thrill ahead. [3]The skateboarder runs his skateboard up the ramp, somersaults in the air, and slams back down at incredible speeds. [4]Many communities frown on skateboarding because of the noise and damage caused to sidewalks and handrails. [5]A young woman stands on the span of a bridge that looms hundreds of feet high. [6]When she jumps, she is counting on her parachute to carry her away from the bridge instead of slamming her into its concrete foundation. [7]She hopes to race toward the ground at speeds over 60 miles an hour, and she plans to pull the cord in just enough time to swoop gently to the ground. [8]She is BASE jumping. [9]Participation in extreme sports like snowboarding, sky diving, ice climbing, skateboarding, and BASE jumping is on the rise.

_____9. Which of the following claims is adequately supported by the evidence?
   a. Extreme sports appeal only to crazy people.
   b. Extreme sports should not be covered by insurance.
   c. Extreme sports attract athletes who want to experience danger and excitement.
   d. Extreme sports should be banned.

_____10. Which sentence is not relevant to the claim?
   a. sentence 1
   b. sentence 3
   c. sentence 4
   d. sentence 9

Name_____ Section _____ Date _____ Score (number correct) _____ x 10 = _____

Objective: To identify the claim and support in an argument.

A. Directions: Read all of the statements for each question and choose the claim.

_____1. Which one of the following sentences states the claim for this group of ideas?
    a. Embalming fluid contains harmful chemicals, antibiotics, dyes, and more, which eventually make their way into the soil, potentially contaminating our water supplies.
    b. More than 1 million gallons of embalming fluid are buried during funerals in the United States every year.
    c. Because traditional burial practices can have a significant negative impact on environment, our country should look for eco-friendly options.
    d. Each year, more than 20,000 cemeteries in the United States bury millions of feet of hardwood; tens of thousands of tons of steel, copper, and bronze; and more than a million tons of reinforced concrete.

_____2. Which one of the following sentences states the claim for this group of ideas?
    a. The organs from one donor can save or help as many as 50 people.
    b. Approximately 79 people receive organ transplants every day.
    c. An average of 18 people die each day waiting for transplants because of the shortage of donated organs.
    d. More people should consider donating their organs.

_____3. Which one of the following sentences states the claim for this group of ideas?
    a. Adequate consumption of calcium throughout one's life can help prevent bone loss in later years.
    b. Vitamin D is necessary for adequate calcium absorption, yet as people age, they do not absorb vitamin D from foods as readily as before.
    c. Paying close attention to diet is especially important for healthy aging.
    d. As some older adults become concerned about cholesterol and fatty foods, they often cut back on protein; however, protein is necessary for muscle mass and protein insufficiencies can spell trouble.

B. Directions: Read the following outline of a point and its supports. Decide if each support is relevant to the claim or if it is not relevant to the claim.

Claim: Cell phone use may be dangerous to your health.

Support:

_____4. Cell phones emit radio frequency energy when turned on.
    a. relevant
    b. not relevant

Support:

_____5. Depending on how close to the phone is to your head, as much as 60 percent of the radio frequency energy penetrates the skull, neck, and upper torso, some of it reaching as far as 1.5 inches into the brain.
     a. relevant
     b. not relevant

Support:

_____6. Cell phones are used by billions of people around the world.
     a. relevant
     b. not relevant

Support:

_____7. U.S. Food and Drug Administration and other major health agencies agree that more research on the dangers of cell phones is needed as it is a relatively new technology and no long-term studies exist.
     a. relevant
     b. not relevant

Support:

_____8. Preliminary results from well-designed but small studies continue to raise questions about the correlation between phone use and tumors.
     a. relevant
     b. not relevant

Support:

_____9. Three large studies compared cellphone use among brain cancer patients and individuals free of brain cancer and found no correlation between phone use and tumors.
     a. relevant
     b. not relevant

Support:

_____10. In the United States, safety standards for cell phone radiation are set by the Federal Communications Commission.
     a. relevant
     b. not relevant

Name_____ Section _____ Date _____ Score (number correct) _____ x 10 = _____

A. Directions: Read all of the statements for each question and choose the claim.

_____1. Which one of the following sentences states the claim for this group of ideas?
    a. Basketball players must be able to sprint up and down the court for two and a half hours.
    b. Basketball has the longest playing season of all the major sports.
    c. Basketball players are some of the best all-round athletes.
    d. Unlike any other athletes, basketball players must use speed, endurance, and accuracy skills at the same time.

_____2. Which one of the following sentences states the claim for this group of ideas?
    a. Many video games encourage violence.
    b. Many violent video games put the player in the role of seeking and killing victims.
    c. Some experts believe that role-playing is an important step in becoming violent.
    d. Other experts fear that the violence in the games makes players think of violence as fun.

_____3. Which one of the following sentences states the claim for this group of ideas?
    a. Marijuana has proven medical benefits for cancer patients.
    b. Marijuana stimulates the appetite and eases the discomfort of those who suffer with nausea from chemotherapy.
    c. Marijuana should be legalized.
    d. The current ban on marijuana has not stopped its sale and use.

B. Directions: Read the following outline of a point and its supports. Decide if each support is relevant to the claim or if it is not relevant to the claim.

Claim: You can improve your study time at home.

Support

_____4. Sit toward the front of the classroom.
    a. relevant
    b. not relevant

_____5. Have supplies nearby, such as paper, pens, pencils, class notes, and textbooks.
    a. relevant
    b. not relevant

_____6. Get rid of external distractions by shutting off the radio and television or moving to a quiet location.
    a. relevant
    b. not relevant

C. Directions: Read the following outline of a point and its supports. Decide if each support is relevant to the claim or if it is not relevant to the claim.

Claim: Meditation is an excellent way to relax and manage stress.

Support

_____7. Meditation uses deep breathing to release tension and relax muscles.
     a.   relevant
     b.   not relevant

Support

_____8. Anyone can practice meditation because it easy to learn and has no cost.
     a.   relevant
     b.   not relevant

Support

_____9. Meditation also turns the mind away from problems and focuses on inner peace.
     a.   relevant
     b.   not relevant

Support

_____10. Many people resist using meditation as a stress-management tool because they think it is a religious practice.
     a.   relevant
     b.   not relevant

Name_____ Section _____ Date _____ Score (number correct) _____ x 10 = _____

Ritalin: Use or Abuse?

Doctors prescribe it, parents pass it out to children, and school nurses supervise the administration of it because all believe the pill will calm children and stop their disruptive behavior. It is methylphenidate. Best known by the brand name Ritalin, methylphenidate was introduced in 1956 and is a stimulant in the same class as amphetamines. Experts agree that it affects the midbrain, the part of the brain that controls impulses.

Advocates of Ritalin assert that the drug is a blessing and that it has helped those with attention deficit/hyperactivity disorder (ADHD) to concentrate. People diagnosed with ADHD are unable to sit still, plan ahead, finish tasks, or be fully aware of what's going on around them. To their family, classmates, or coworkers, they seem to exist in a cyclone of disorganized or harried activity. One of the most common mental disorders among children, it affects 3% to 5% of all children, perhaps as many as 2 million children in the United States. Two to three times more boys than girls are affected, and on average, at least one child in every classroom in the United States needs help for the disorder.

Ritalin allows the patient to focus better on the task at hand. Besides its use in treating the symptoms of ADHD, Ritalin is also prescribed for mild to moderate depression and in some cases of emotional withdrawal among elderly people. Initially Ritalin was used for children who were so restless that they were unreachable and unteachable. The National Institutes of Health support "the efficacy of stimulants and psychosocial treatments for ADHD and the superiority of stimulants relative to psychosocial treatments." The benefits of Ritalin are so strong that advocates say withholding the pills is a form of neglect. Those who claim diet, exercise, or other treatments work just as well are kidding themselves, say believers. A typical parental comment is the following:

> His homework took 3 hours—even with me helping him—to do because his mind was in the sky. He was a genius at video games, but not at homework. He was also at the point of being held back in school. He shed tears because he could not control himself; he hated the way he acted. I was always getting complaints about his spontaneous outbursts. And then he took Ritalin—and everything changed.

But the situation is not all rosy. Critics say doctors who work with teachers to keep boisterous children in line misdiagnose students. As awareness of ADHD has grown, the characterization of the disorder now encompasses a much broader range of behaviors—an increasing number of children seem to have conditions that meet the definition of ADHD.

Ritalin production has increased by more than 700% since 1990. Since then disorders for which Ritalin is prescribed have jumped an average of 21% per year. Over the past five years alone, the number of prescriptions for Ritalin in the United States has jumped to 11.4 million from 4.5 million, including about 11% of all boys in the United States. Researchers claim a disturbing reliance upon the drug to solve problems that have other solutions.

Ritalin is classified as a Schedule II drug—on a par with cocaine, morphine, and methamphetamines—thus there is potential for abuse or dependence. Ritalin is widely misused by drug addicts, and it has associated with it a large number of suicides and emergency room admissions. The National Institutes of Health caution that "stimulant treatments may not 'normalize' the entire range of behavior problems, and children under treatment may still manifest a higher level of some behavior problems than normal children." They also note that there are no long-term studies testing stimulants or psychosocial treatments lasting several years.

Of course, an ADHD diagnosis can and often does lead to medication, special education facilities, and parental support groups. Today, children and teenagers with ADHD may be placed in a special classroom and eventually get non-timed college admission tests—about 40,000 SAT tests are administered this way each year. Are the ADHD diagnosis and the Ritalin treatment being used for the wrong reasons? By overzealous parents? By well-meaning physicians?

Is Ritalin effective? Yes, it is. Can it help children and teenagers with ADHD? Yes, it can. Are mistakes made in diagnosing ADHD? Of course. Is there over-diagnosis? Yes. Over-diagnosis usually occurs when a doctor is inexperienced, untrained, pressured, or predisposed to "find" ADHD. We need careful controlled research into the impact and long-term effects of Ritalin—and those studies are still a few years away. We also need physician, teacher, and parent education into ADHD and the use of Ritalin.

—Lofton & Brannon, *Psychology*, 8th ed., pp. 100–101.

_____ 1. The topic of the passage is _____.
- a. reasons Ritalin should continue to be prescribed by physicians
- b. reasons Ritalin should not continue to be prescribed by physicians
- c. the advantages and disadvantages of Ritalin
- d. the increase in hyperactivity in the U.S. population

_____ 2. The purpose of the passage is to _____.
- a. persuade parents to seek professional help for their hyperactive children
- b. inform people of the positive and negative aspects of Ritalin
- c. persuade physicians to exercise caution when prescribing Ritalin
- d. inform adults about the misuses of Ritalin

_____ 3. The claim of the argument advanced in the passage is that _____.
- a. conflicting information about the benefits and problems of Ritalin use indicate that more study and caution are required
- b. critics of the use of Ritalin should rethink their position, since there are so many advantages to using the drug
- c. proponents of Ritalin use have failed to consider the disadvantages of the drug
- d. people should learn self-discipline and alternate methods of handling hyperactivity, rather than relying on Ritalin, which is viewed as a dangerous "quick fix"

_____ 4. The audience to which this selection is aimed would include all of the following *except* _____.
- a. pediatricians
- b. educators
- c. parents
- d. entertainers

_____5. "Ritalin allows the patient to focus better on the task at hand."
    a. This statement is relevant to the claim.
    b. This statement is not relevant to the claim.

_____6. "Besides its use in treating the symptoms of ADHD, Ritalin is also prescribed for mild to moderate depression and in some cases of emotional withdrawal among elderly people."
    a. This statement is relevant to the claim.
    b. This statement is not relevant to the claim.

_____7. "Initially Ritalin was used for children who were so restless that they were unreachable and unteachable."
    a. This statement is relevant to the claim.
    b. This statement is not relevant to the claim.

_____8. "The National Institutes of Health support 'the efficacy of stimulants and psychosocial treatments for ADHD and the superiority of stimulants relative to psychosocial treatments.'"
    a. This statement is relevant to the claim.
    b. This statement is not relevant to the claim.

_____9. "The benefits of Ritalin are so strong that advocates say withholding the pills is a form of neglect."
    a. This statement is relevant to the claim.
    b. This statement is not relevant to the claim.

_____10. "Those who claim diet, exercise, or other treatments work just as well are kidding themselves, say believers."
    a. This statement is relevant to the claim.
    b. This statement is not relevant to the claim.

Name _____ Section _____ Date _____ Score (number correct) _____ x 10 = _____

A. Directions: Read all of the statements for each question and choose the claim.

_____1. Which one of the following sentences states the claim for this group of ideas?
   a. Nuclear power plants account for less than 1 percent of the total radiation to which we are currently exposed.
   b. Nuclear reactors discharge fewer carbon oxides into the air than do fossil fuel-powered generators.
   c. A 1,000 megawatt reactor produces enough energy for 650,000 homes and saves 420 million gallons of fossil fuels each year.
   d. Nuclear power plants are an efficient and safe source for generating electricity.

_____2. Which one of the following sentences states the claim for this group of ideas?
   a. Disposal of nuclear waste is very difficult and problematic.
   b. A reactor core meltdown poses serious threats to the immediate environment and to the world in general.
   c. To date, the world has seen two major nuclear disasters that caused a major release of radioactive material with widespread health and environmental consequences.
   d. Nuclear power plants should not be allowed.

_____3. Which one of the following sentences states the claim for this group of ideas?
   a. Gangs give members a sense of self-worth, companionship, security, and excitement.
   b. Gangs provide economic security as a result of their illegal activities.
   c. Gangs meet many of the personal needs of young people.
   d. Teens with low self-esteem, academic problems, low socioeconomic status, and alienation from family and society often find acceptance in gangs.

_____4. Which one of the following sentences states the claim for this group of ideas?
   a. Estimates indicate that between 700,000 and 3.5 million older Americans may be abused, neglected, or exploited each year.
   b. Many elderly citizens suffer from dementia and are vulnerable to abuse.
   c. Our nation is guilty of not providing properly for its elderly citizens.
   d. Elderly citizens who are socially isolated are more likely to suffer from abuse.

B. Directions: Read the following outline of a point and its supports. Decide if each support is relevant to the claim or if it is not relevant to the claim.

Claim: Continued climate change will disrupt ecosystems and endanger many species.

Support

____5. Based on current models, average global temperature will rise by at least 3.2 degrees to as much as 7.2 degrees by the year 2100.
      a. relevant
      b. not relevant

Support

____6. Because of warmer temperatures, thousands of species will change their ranges, which will leave many without a food supply.
      a. relevant
      b. not relevant

Support

____7. Currently there are almost 2 million known living species that exist in our world.
      a. relevant
      b. not relevant

Support

____8. Some species, particularly those on mountains or in the Arctic and Antarctic, will have nowhere to go as the climate warms, consequently dying out.
      a. relevant
      b. not relevant

Support

____9. Complete loss of sea ice, which climate models predict could occur within the next century, may cause the extinction of wild polar bears, whose habitat depends on the ice.
      a. relevant
      b. not relevant

Support

____10. Both engineering and biological approaches to reverse global warming have been proposed.
      a. relevant
      b. not relevant

Name_____ Section _____ Date _____ Score (number correct) _____ x 10 = _____

A. Directions: Read all of the statements for each question and choose the claim.

_____1. Which one of the following sentences states the claim for this group of ideas?
   a. A recent study by the Partnership for a Drug-Free America showed that 45 percent of youths aged 12 to 18 saw a great risk in using the drug Ecstasy.
   b. In 2001, over 5,000 emergency-room visits were related to Ecstasy use.
   c. In 2002, 253 emergency-room visits were related to Ecstasy use.
   d. Although many teenagers see the risk of using Ecstasy, the dangers the drug poses to youth should not be ignored.

_____2. Which one of the following sentences states the claim for this group of ideas?
   a. Never rely solely on eyewitness accounts, which can be biased or faulty.
   b. You should use these guidelines to help you decide when an employee should be fired for theft.
   c. Meet with the accused to get all the facts; there may be a reasonable explanation.
   d. Weigh the employee's offense against other disciplinary problems to avoid a harsh overreaction.

_____3. Which one of the following sentences states the claim for this group of ideas?
   a. Cloning is an imperfect scientific process that can result in problems in the cloned animals.
   b. Most attempts at cloning end in failure because the fetuses have oversized organs in the womb or are born stillborn.
   c. Other cloned animals have been born twice as large as normal.
   d. A veterinary exam confirmed that a 6-year-old cloned sheep had a progressive lung disease.

_____4. Which one of the following sentences states the claim for this group of ideas adapted from the college text, DeVito, *Messages: Building Interpersonal Communication Skills,* 4th ed., p. 331?
   a. Sexual harassment in school has harmful effects on students who are victims.
   b. Students who have been victims of sexual harassment in school have trouble paying attention, have trouble studying, and earn low grades.
   c. Many of these students have difficulty speaking out in class, don't want to go to school, or think about changing schools.
   d. Victims of sexual harassment are often too afraid to speak to policemen.

B. Directions: Read the paragraphs and answer the questions that follow.

[1]Have you noticed that mounting malpractice insurance costs have pressured doctors to limit their time with patients by requiring an allotted number of face-to-face office visits a day? [2]Insurance companies have acquired an inordinate amount of power that affects everyone, a situation that now calls for a dramatic change. [3]The high cost of malpractice insurance has actually prompted some doctors to leave medicine and find jobs in other fields. [4]Some doctors have turned to law, while others have left the professional ranks altogether. [5]Also, as a result of rising insurance costs and a reduction in the services some companies cover, many patients postpone or cancel needed exams or procedures.

_____5. Which sentence states the claim of the argument?
    a. sentence 1
    b. sentence 2
    c. sentence 3
    d. sentence 4

_____6. Which sentence is *not* a valid support for the claim?
    a. sentence 2
    b. sentence 3
    c. sentence 4
    d. sentence 5

[1]Creating a new reservoir in the eastern part of the state will reduce the shad population, which is an important contributor to the state's economic growth. [2]As it now stands, the proposal for a new reservoir would have a negative impact on the entire state. [3]It would displace many people from their homes. [4]It would also destroy important Indian ancestral land, including the burial grounds for the Mattaponi Indians. [5]Real estate prices would rise in the area, contributing dollars to the needed tax base.

_____7. Which sentence states the claim of the argument?
    a. sentence 1
    b. sentence 2
    c. sentence 3
    d. sentence 4

_____8. Which sentence is *not* a valid support for the claim?
    a. sentence 2
    b. sentence 3
    c. sentence 4
    d. sentence 5

[1]The traffic signal at the junction of Main Trail and Granada Boulevard makes the intersection dangerous. [2]Whoever programmed the light is stupid. [3]Granada Boulevard is a heavily traveled four-lane state road. [4]Main Trail is the entrance to a large residential neighborhood. [5]To enter the neighborhood, traffic must turn left. [6]The traffic signal is programmed to turn green and allow the left turn into the neighborhood. [7]However, after only two or three cars turn, the left turn signal turns red. [8]Cars are forced to wait at the red light long after there is no more oncoming traffic. [9]To avoid sitting through a five-minute red light, many drivers rush through the signal as it turns yellow or run the light after it has turned red. [10]The timing of the light encourages reckless driving.

_____9. Which sentence states the claim of the argument?
      a.   sentence 1
      b.   sentence 2
      c.   sentence 3
      d.   sentence 4

_____10. Which sentence is NOT a valid support for the claim?
      a.   sentence 2
      b.   sentence 4
      c.   sentence 7
      d.   sentence 9

185

Name_____ Section _____ Date _____ Score (number correct) _____ x 10 = _____

Objective: To identify fallacies of logic and propaganda techniques.

A. Directions: Choose the fallacy used in each of the following items.

_____1. I like R & B music, because it's my favorite.
   a. begging the question
   b. personal attack
   c. straw man
   d. either-or

_____2. My record is the record and it represents my excellence in the field because it is so good.
   a. begging the question
   b. personal attack
   c. straw man
   d. either-or

_____3. Why would anyone vote for that candidate? He is an overzealous tree-hugger who hasn't a clue about how to run a government.
   a. begging the question
   b. personal attack
   c. straw man
   d. either-or

_____4. Paul is a generous and courageous man because he is a fire fighter, and all fire fighters are brave.
   a. begging the question
   b. personal attack
   c. straw man
   d. either-or

_____5. Governor Rock Slide is an excellent politician because he is also a movie star.
   a. begging the question
   b. personal attack
   c. straw man
   d. either-or

B. Directions: Identify the propaganda technique used in each of the following items.

_____ 6. Are you tired of being told what to do? Do you want a venue that is safe for expressing your own views? Come join the Young Democrats and hook up with open-minded, progressive-thinking members.
   a. plain folk
   b. bandwagon
   c. testimonial
   d. name-calling

_____ 7. "Ever since I started eating Maine blueberries, I've had more energy and more clarity of thought. There is nothing better than the natural properties of this home-grown product, and I promise you will enjoy similar benefits as well."
   a. plain folk
   b. bandwagon
   c. testimonial
   d. name-calling

_____ 8. The advertisement displays two sandwiches. One is a large, juicy double cheeseburger. The other is a small, flat burger on a bun. The caption reads, "Theirs? Ours? You decide."
   a. plain folk
   b. bandwagon
   c. testimonial
   d. name-calling

_____ 9. Mr. Santiago works diligently in his yard each weekend to touch up the paint on the house, clean the gutters, rake the yard, plant flowers, and wash windows. Recently he said, "I have pride in my home, and I work hard to make sure it looks good so that it is a reflection of the order in my personal life."
   a. transfer
   b. glittering generalities
   c. card stacking
   d. testimonial

_____ 10. A representative of a computer software firm offers a presentation on his company's product and explains that using the program for a college's student information system will facilitate record-keeping and provide opportunities for online registration. He also mentions that the program has been used successfully in many businesses across the country. However, he fails to tell the group that the company is currently in litigation with the community college system in another state because it did not dovetail easily to the academic arena and had previously only been an effective human resource program for some national businesses.
   a. transfer
   b. glittering generalities
   c. card stacking
   d. bandwagon

Name_____ Section _____ Date _____ Score (number correct) _____ x 10 = _____

Objective: To identify fallacies of logic and propaganda techniques.

A. Directions: Choose the fallacy used in each of the following items.

_____1. If we believe our society should help people in unfortunate circumstances, then we should support the national health care plan completely. The only other option is to completely turn our backs on those who can't help themselves.
    a. begging the question
    b. personal attack
    c. straw man
    d. either-or

_____2. Shows like Honey Boo Boo and Toddlers & Tiaras show the worst of human behavior and should be removed from television because we don't need to see humans behaving stupidly.
    a. begging the question
    b. personal attack
    c. straw man
    d. false cause

_____3. That handsome man who is running for mayor is sadly more famous for his drug use and illicit affairs than for his ability to lead a community.
    a. begging the question
    b. personal attack
    c. straw man
    d. false comparison

_____4. Either choose to fight back for what you believe in, or do nothing and live in misery.
    a. either-or
    b. begging the question
    b. personal attack
    c. straw man

_____5. Our schools have become dehumanizing jails. Students are just as mistreated by the education system as prisoners are when locked up into those stifling cells.
    a. begging the question
    b. personal attack
    c. straw man
    d. false comparison

B. Directions: Identify the propaganda technique used in each of the following items.

_____6. Don't be the only one without a Facebook page. How else will all your classmates find you?
      a. name-calling
      b. testimonial
      c. band wagon
      d. transfer

_____7. Mary Ann was awarded the highest honor ever given to a principal of a school. Through her leadership, the school's performance records for achievement have risen dramatically in all areas. Mary Ann is also a leader in her church and in her community, and she teaches an evening class at the local college. In addition, she supervises student teachers through their first experience in the classroom. We could not possibly find anyone better suited for the position of school superintendent.
      a. glittering generalities
      b. testimonial
      c. card stacking
      d. band wagon

_____8. Although he comes from an extremely wealthy family and did not grow up in our state, our senator can often be seen walking around small towns without a jacket or tie and with his shirt sleeves rolled up to the elbows. He often stops to greet the townspeople and to encourage them to discuss their opinions about the effects of coal mining on the town.
      a. plain folks
      b. name-calling
      c. glittering generalities
      d. transfer

_____9. Nike products must be the best because so many professional players endorse them.
      a. testimonial
      b. glittering generalities
      c. plain folks
      d. transfer

_____10. The slogan for Macy's department store "The Magic of Macy's" suggests that all shoppers will have an enchanting and magical experience while shopping in Macy's.
      a. name-calling
      b. plain folks
      c. glittering generalities
      d. testimonial

Name_____ Section _____ Date _____ Score (number correct) _____ x 10 = _____

A. Directions: Identify the fallacy used in each of the following items.

_____1. Although the drainage ditches in our residential areas are unsightly and unhealthy, local officials refuse to authorize city workers to lay drainage pipes to fill them in because they don't care about issues that affect the environment.
  a. begging the question
  b. personal attack
  c. straw man
  d. false comparison

_____2. The play was replete with profanity, and it is obvious that the theater department intends to undermine the family values in our community.
  a. begging the question
  b. personal attack
  c. straw man
  d. either-or

_____3. Consumers who buy fur and leather products are nothing but a bunch of hypocrites who have no respect for nature.
  a. begging the question
  b. personal attack
  c. straw man
  d. false comparison

_____4. Currently there is a six-year waiting list for anyone with a mental disability to move into a group home. Why are our state politicians more concerned about providing tax cuts for the rich than helping those in need?
  a. false cause
  b. personal attack
  c. either-or
  d. straw man

_____5. President Smith eliminated four major programs at our college so he could fund the building of new dormitories and landscape the grounds with fountains and flowers. He is clearly looking out for himself and does not care about this institution; he wants only to pad his résumé, so he can run a successful campaign for governor.
  a. personal attack
  b. begging the question
  c. either-or
  d. false comparison

191

B. Directions: Identify the propaganda technique used in each of the following items.

_____6. The automobile advertisement displaying a woman in work clothes states: "This is Eleanor. She is a mother and a grandmother. She is also one of our assembly-line technicians, and her job is to make sure our cars are safe for her parents, for her children, and for YOU."
   a. plain folks
   b. bandwagon
   c. testimonial
   d. name-calling

_____7. The advertisement displays a photograph of Olympic swimmers from four countries as they wait on deck, listening to music using the same earphones and CD player. The caption reads: "Join the winners. Own one, too!"
   a. plain folks
   b. glittering generalities
   c. testimonial
   d. name-calling

_____8. "He lied in college. He lied in law school. He lied in the Pentagon in 1990. And he lied to you last year. Ah, that must be what the "L" stands for in John L. Farber. A vote for me is a vote for honesty."
   a. plain folks
   b. bandwagon
   c. testimonial
   d. name-calling

_____9. A young man appears at your door with a clipboard in hand and says, "All of your neighbors have signed this petition to endorse speed bumps on the neighborhood streets. You don't want to be left out, do you?"
   a. plain folks
   b. bandwagon
   c. testimonial
   d. name-calling

C. Directions: Read the following fictitious advertisement. Identify the detail that was **omitted** from the advertisement for the purpose of card-stacking.

_____10. Blue Oasis is the most refreshing bottled water on the market. Not only does it quench your thirst, but it will also compensate for any mineral deficiencies your body may have. Enjoy the guarantee that you are drinking our safe, clean, and untainted water that is cleansed by nature's own best purifier— from the underground springs and rocks through which it flows. For generations, our water has been particularly linked to health and well-being.
   a. Drinking water helps to keep the body hydrated.
   b. Bottled water is less regulated than tap water. There are few if any restrictions on it.
   c. Water is a far better choice for children than drinks sweetened with sugar.
   d. Water plays an essential role in good hydration before and after heavy exercise.

Name_____ Section _____ Date _____ Score (number correct) _____ x 10 = _____

A. Directions: Identify the fallacy used in each of the following items.

_____1. Our senator is a proponent of building a stronger navy and increasing the number of nuclear submarines, which means that he is more interested in serving his constituents than ensuring that we focus on world peace.
   a. begging the question
   b. personal attack
   c. straw man
   d. either-or

_____2. The mayor is a known womanizer, so how can we trust him to provide leadership in our city?
   a. begging the question
   b. personal attack
   c. straw man
   d. either-or

_____3. Athletes should be given special treatment on campus because they are students worthy of extra benefits.
   a. begging the question
   b. personal attack
   c. straw man
   d. either-or

_____4. How can you say you have grown up? Look at the way you spend your money, always buying expensive toys and impractical vehicles!
   a. begging the question
   b. personal attack
   c. straw man
   d. either-or

_____5. Circumventing the law is not unethical if it is legal.
   a. begging the question
   b. personal attack
   c. straw man
   d. either-or

193

B. Directions: Identify the propaganda technique used in each of the following items.

_____ 6. When orchestrating his candidate's photo shoot, a campaign manager staged the family in front of a tree in the front yard, rather than on the back deck that overlooked the river. He then had his candidate remove his gold cuff links and Rolex watch, roll up his sleeves, and shoot some baskets with his sons. He was using which strategy to promote his candidate?
   a. plain folk
   b. bandwagon
   c. testimonial
   d. name-calling

_____ 7. Before the interview with the presidential candidate, the camera captures him running barefoot on a public beach with his dog and children nearby. He wears rolled up khaki pants, a wrinkled blue work shirt, and an Atlanta Braves ball cap. This photo shoot uses which strategy?
   a. plain folk
   b. bandwagon
   c. testimonial
   d. name-calling

_____ 8. A local TV station calls a water theme park supervisor to apprise the management that they secretly took a water sample of their pool and discovered the chlorine levels there are dangerously low and they are planning to air an expose of the business. What they will not mention in their report, however, is that chlorine burns off in sunlight, and their sample was exposed for three hours outside before it was tested.
   a. transfer
   b. glittering generalities
   c. card stacking
   d. bandwagon

_____ 9. If he were still here, Ronald Reagan would have supported our efforts to expand stem-cell research.
   a. transfer
   b. glittering generalities
   c. card stacking
   d. bandwagon

_____ 10. It is my privilege to introduce our company president—the go-to guy, the man of decisive action and vision, the man who seeks solutions. Because of his leadership, our corporation has become a world class organization.
   a. transfer
   b. glittering generalities
   c. card stacking
   d. plain folks

Name_____ Section _____ Date _____ Score (number correct) _____ x 10 = _____

A. Directions: Identify the fallacy used in each of the following items.

_____1. Jogging is one of the best exercises possible because running works out all of the body's muscles.
    a. false cause
    b. begging the question
    c. either-or
    d. straw man

_____2. I lost a tooth after the birth of each of my children. Pregnancy causes the loss of teeth.
    a. false comparison
    b. straw man
    c. false cause
    d. either-or

_____3. Marriage is just like a business. The partners always have to pay attention to the bottom line.
    a. straw man
    b. false cause
    c. begging the question
    d. false comparison

_____4. If you believe in saving the environment, you will make a donation to support our cause. Otherwise you are not a friend of the earth.
    a. straw man
    b. false cause
    c. false comparison
    d. either-or

_____5. Those young men look like gangsters. They are covered in tattoos, and they look unkempt. They are clearly looking for trouble.
    a. false comparison
    b. straw man
    c. false cause
    d. either-or

B. Directions: Identify the propaganda technique used in each of the following items.

_____6. Many men purchased a Rolex watch after seeing famous golfer, Phil Mickelson, wearing one on television.
    a. transfer
    b. glittering generalities
    c. name-calling
    d. plain folks

_____7. Levi Strauss ads urge the young to "Seize the Day!" If they wear Levis they will be ready to "take on the world!"
   a. transfer
   b. testimonial
   c. bandwagon
   d. glittering generalities

_____8. All teenagers know that if they aren't wearing the "in" fashions worn by all the "cool" students, they won't be considered "in!"
   a. testimonial
   b. transfer
   c. glittering generalities
   d. bandwagon

_____9. Christian Bale, the main actor in *Batman*, always wore a classy suit in his Batman movie, similar to one that he endorses in a Giorgio Armani ad. Obviously this is an intelligent superstar who believes in the value of the prestigious and high-class Armani clothing line.
   a. testimonial
   b. plain folks
   c. glittering generalities
   d. bandwagon

C. Directions: Read the following fictitious advertisement. Identify the detail that was **omitted** from the advertisement for the purpose of card stacking.

_____10. Electronic cigarettes (e-cigarettes) are a good alternative for smokers. E-cigarettes do not have that horrible odor that regular cigarettes have. E-cigarettes aren't nearly as expensive as regular cigarettes. Finally, traditional cigarettes pose serious fire hazards, but there is no flame in an e-cigarrette. Make the switch to electronic cigarettes!

   a. E-cigarrettes emit a vapor that evaporates almost immediately, so they smell much better than regular cigarettes.
   b. Currently e-cigarettes are not taxed like traditional cigarettes are, so they are much cheaper.
   c. E-cigarettes can't claim to be healthier, but everyone knows how harmful traditional cigarettes are to everyone's health.
   d. Smokers with a pack-a-day habit can spend close to $300 a month, while smoking e-cigrarettes may cost around $40 to $60 a month.

CHAPTER 13: ADVANCED ARGUMENT: PERSUASIVE TECHNIQUES
Lab 13.6 MASTERY TEST 2

Name_____ Section_____ Date_____ Score (number correct)_____ x 10 = _____

A. Directions: Identify the fallacy used in each of the following items.

____1. If you don't shop with us, you might as well throw your money away. Only here are you guaranteed to save three cents on every dollar. Shop with us, or lose out on the best deal in town.
   a. either-or
   b. straw man
   c. false cause
   d. false comparison

____2. Laws are to society what discipline is in the home. Just as children do not understand all the reasons for each and every rule in the house, citizens do not have to understand all the reasons a good law is needed.
   a. begging the question
   b. false cause
   c. false comparison
   d. straw man

____3. Those who oppose a minimum wage fear the success of others.
   a. personal attack
   b. false comparison
   c. either-or
   d. begging the question

____4. The lack of a minimum wage acts upon our society like a cancerous disease destroying the economic health of millions of families.
   a. begging the question
   b. false cause
   c. either-or
   d. false comparison

____5. Celine Ortega supports stem-cell research just to get the votes of families whose loved ones suffer with disabilities and diseases such as Alzheimers.
   a. false comparison
   b. false cause
   c. personal attack
   d. straw man

B. Directions: Identify the propaganda technique used in each of the following items.

_____6. Dale Earnhardt Jr. drives a car sponsored by Budweiser in the NASCAR races.
      a. bandwagon
      b. transfer
      c. plain folks
      d. glittering generalities

_____7. Buy SureGrip hammers. These hammers are the best, and they were designed with you and all your everyday household needs in mind.
      a. card stacking
      b. name-calling
      c. plain folks
      d. glittering generalities

_____8. We condemn the cowardly and dastardly attack upon the Flag of the United States and the Pledge of Allegiance by Cita Zen, a traitor of all that is decent.
      a. name calling
      b. testimonial
      c. plain folks
      d. glittering generalities

_____9. I do not seek public office out of the need for power; indeed I take up the cross of service with the humility of one who is called to fulfill a holy mission.
      a. transfer
      b. bandwagon
      c. name-calling
      d. plain folks

C. Directions: Read the following fictitious advertisement. Identify the detail that was **omitted** from the advertisement for the purpose of card-stacking.

_____10. Everyone should have a Jack Russell terrier. The Jack Russell is a happy, bold, and energetic dog. These dogs are extremely loyal and intelligent. The dogs make great pets as they harbor all the wonderful traits of man's best friend. You can see for yourself the endearing qualities of the Jack Russell, Eddie, on the popular sitcom *Frasier*. Since this show has been aired, the popularity of Jack Russells has increased remarkably.
      a. Jack Russells are incredibly loving and devoted.
      b. Jack Russells are little dogs that can fit easily into a small apartment.
      c. Jack Russells are relatively smart dogs and easy to train.
      d. Jack Russells need a lot of exercise, which includes a minimum of a one-hour walk and several hours of play each day.

SCORE SHEETS FOR PRACTICE TESTS

FLORIDA COLLEGE BASIC SKILLS EXIT READING TEST

TEXAS HIGHER EDUCATION ASSESSMENT TEST

THE EFFECTIVE READER

AWARENESS INVENTORIES

FLORIDA COLLEGE BASIC SKILLS EXIT TEST

TEXAS HIGHER EDUCATION ASSESSMENT TEST

DIAGNOSTIC TEST FOR *THE EFFECTIVE READER*

SUMMARY SHEET OF SCORES

Name _____ Date _____

Objective: To practice for the *Florida College Basic Skills Exit Reading Test*.

Take the practice test, *Florida College Basic Skills Exit Reading Test*, in your textbook. Fill in the correct answer for each numbered item. Be sure to choose only one answer for each numbered item.

_____ 1. _____ 15. _____ 28.

_____ 2. _____ 16. _____ 29.

_____ 3. _____ 17. _____ 30.

_____ 4. _____ 18. _____ 31.

_____ 5. _____ 19. _____ 32.

_____ 6. _____ 20. _____ 33.

_____ 7. _____ 21. _____ 34.

_____ 8. _____ 22. _____ 35.

_____ 9. _____ 23. _____ 36.

_____ 10. _____ 24. _____ 37.

_____ 11. _____ 25. _____ 38.

_____ 12. _____ 26. _____ 39.

_____ 13. _____ 27. _____ 40.

_____ 14.

Name _____ Date _____

Objective: To gain more practice for the *Florida College Basic Skills Exit Reading Test*.

Fill in the correct answer for each numbered item. Be sure to choose only one answer for each numbered item.

_____ 1. _____ 15. _____ 28.

_____ 2. _____ 16. _____ 29.

_____ 3. _____ 17. _____ 30.

_____ 4. _____ 18. _____ 31.

_____ 5. _____ 19. _____ 32.

_____ 6. _____ 20. _____ 33.

_____ 7. _____ 21. _____ 34.

_____ 8. _____ 22. _____ 35.

_____ 9. _____ 23. _____ 36.

_____ 10. _____ 24. _____ 37.

_____ 11. _____ 25. _____ 38.

_____ 12. _____ 26. _____ 39.

_____ 13. _____ 27. _____ 40.

_____ 14.

PRACTICE TEST FOR THE TEXAS HIGHER EDUCATION ASSESSMENT TEST

Name _____ Date _____

Objective: To practice for the *Texas Higher Education Assessment Test*.

Take the practice test, *Texas Higher Education Assessment Test*, in your textbook. Fill in the correct answer for each numbered item. Be sure to choose only one answer for each numbered item.

_____ 1. _____ 15. _____ 28.

_____ 2. _____ 16. _____ 29.

_____ 3. _____ 17. _____ 30.

_____ 4. _____ 18. _____ 31.

_____ 5. _____ 19. _____ 32.

_____ 6. _____ 20. _____ 33.

_____ 7. _____ 21. _____ 34.

_____ 8. _____ 22. _____ 35.

_____ 9. _____ 23. _____ 36.

_____ 10. _____ 24. _____ 37.

_____ 11. _____ 25. _____ 38.

_____ 12. _____ 26. _____ 39.

_____ 13. _____ 27. _____ 40.

_____ 14.

Name _____ Date _____

Objective: To gain more practice for the *Texas Higher Education Assessment Test*.

Fill in the correct answer for each numbered item. Be sure to choose only one answer for each numbered item.

_____ 1. _____ 15. _____ 28.

_____ 2. _____ 16. _____ 29.

_____ 3. _____ 17. _____ 30.

_____ 4. _____ 18. _____ 31.

_____ 5. _____ 19. _____ 32.

_____ 6. _____ 20. _____ 33.

_____ 7. _____ 21. _____ 34.

_____ 8. _____ 22. _____ 35.

_____ 9. _____ 23. _____ 36.

_____ 10. _____ 24. _____ 37.

_____ 11. _____ 25. _____ 38.

_____ 12. _____ 26. _____ 39.

_____ 13. _____ 27. _____ 40.

_____ 14.

Name _____ Date _____

Objective: To discover strengths and areas for improvement in reading comprehension and critical reading.

Take the practice test for *The Effective Reader*, in your textbook. Fill in the correct answer for each numbered item. Be sure to choose only one answer for each numbered item.

_____ 1. _____ 15. _____ 28.

_____ 2. _____ 16. _____ 29.

_____ 3. _____ 17. _____ 30.

_____ 4. _____ 18. _____ 31.

_____ 5. _____ 19. _____ 32.

_____ 6. _____ 20. _____ 33.

_____ 7. _____ 21. _____ 34.

_____ 8. _____ 22. _____ 35.

_____ 9. _____ 23. _____ 36.

_____ 10. _____ 24. _____ 37.

_____ 11. _____ 25. _____ 38.

_____ 12. _____ 26. _____ 39.

_____ 13. _____ 27. _____ 40.

_____ 14.

Name _____ Date _____

Objective: To discover strengths and areas for improvement in reading comprehension and critical reading.

Fill in the correct answer for each numbered item. Be sure to choose only one answer for each numbered item.

_____ 1. _____ 15. _____ 28.

_____ 2. _____ 16. _____ 29.

_____ 3. _____ 17. _____ 30.

_____ 4. _____ 18. _____ 31.

_____ 5. _____ 19. _____ 32.

_____ 6. _____ 20. _____ 33.

_____ 7. _____ 21. _____ 34.

_____ 8. _____ 22. _____ 35.

_____ 9. _____ 23. _____ 36.

_____ 10. _____ 24. _____ 37.

_____ 11. _____ 25. _____ 38.

_____ 12. _____ 26. _____ 39.

_____ 13. _____ 27. _____ 40.

_____ 14.

Name _____ Date _____

Scores: % Correct   % Correct

Passage A   _____   Passage E   _____

Passage B   _____   Passage F   _____

Passage C   _____   Passage G   _____

Passage D   _____

The Reading Section of the *Florida State Basic Skills Exit Test* is based on the skills listed below. Circle the number of questions that you missed. Locate pages in your textbook that will help you develop each specific skill. Write out a study plan.

Passage/Question #	Skill
A4, A5, D6, E4, F4, G3	**Determine the meaning of words and phrases.**
AI, A7, CI, D2, EI, E4, GI, G6, FI, F2	**Understand the main idea and supporting details in written material.**
A2, A3, B2, B3, C2, D3, D5, E2, F3, G2, G5	**Identify a writer's purpose, point of view, and intended meaning.**
A6, DI, E3, F5	**Analyze the relationship among ideas in written material.**
B4, C3, D4, G4	**Use critical reasoning skills to evaluate written material.**
BI, F7	**Apply study skills to reading assignments.**

Plan of Action:

_____

_____

_____

_____

_____

_____

_____

_____

_____

_____

_____

_____

_____

_____

_____

_____

_____

_____

_____

Name _____ Date _____

Scores: % Correct   % Correct

Passage A   _____   Passage E   _____

Passage B   _____   Passage F   _____

Passage C   _____   Passage G   _____

Passage D   _____

The Reading Section of the THEA Test is based on the skills listed below. Circle the number of questions that you missed. Locate pages in your textbook that will help you develop each specific skill. Write out a study plan.

Passage/Question #	Skill
A4, A5, D6, E4, F4, G3	**Determine the meaning of words and phrases.**
AI, A7, CI, D2, EI, E4, GI, G6, FI, F2	**Understand the main idea and supporting details in written material.**
A2, A3, B2, B3, C2, D3, D5, E2, F3, G2, G5	**Identify a writer's purpose, point of view, and intended meaning.**
A6, DI, E3, F5	**Analyze the relationship among ideas in written material.**
B4, C3, D4, G4	**Use critical reasoning skills to evaluate written material.**
BI, F7	**Apply study skills to reading assignments.**

Plan of Action:

_____

_____

_____

_____

_____

_____

_____

_____

_____

_____

_____

_____

_____

_____

_____

_____

_____

Name _____ Date _____

Scores:	% Correct		% Correct
Passage A	_____	Passage C	_____
Passage B	_____	Passage D	_____

The Diagnostic Test for *The Effective Reader* is based on the skills listed below. Circle the number of questions that you missed. Locate pages in your textbook that will help you develop each specific skill. Write out a study plan.

Passage/Question #	Skill	Textbook Pages
A6, A7, B7, B8, C1, D5, D6	**Vocabulary**	_____
A1, A8, B2, C2, C4, D1	**Main idea**	_____
C3, C10, D9	**Supporting Details**	_____
A3, A4, B3, C6	**Thought Patterns**	_____
A5, B5, B6, C5, D7	**Transitions**	_____
A2, A9, C8, C9	**Tone and Purpose**	_____
A9, C7, D8	**Fact/Opinion**	_____
A10, B10, D2, D3, D4	**Inferences**	_____

Plan of Action:

_____

_____

_____

_____

_____

_____

_____

_____

_____

_____

_____

_____

_____

_____

_____

_____

_____

_____

SUMMARY SHEET OF SCORES

	SCORE
Chapter 1: A Reading System for Effective Readers	
Lab 1.1 Practice Exercise 1	
Lab 1.2 Practice Exercise 2	
Lab 1.3 Review Test 1	
Lab 1.4 Review Test 2	
Lab 1.5 Mastery Test 1	
Lab 1.6 Mastery Test 2	
Chapter 2: Vocabulary and Dictionary Skills	
Lab 2.1 Practice Exercise 1	
Lab 2.2 Practice Exercise 2	
Lab 2.3 Review Test 1	
Lab 2.4 Review Test 2	
Lab 2.5 Mastery Test 1	
Lab 2.6 Mastery Test 2	
Chapter 3: Stated Main Ideas	
Lab 3.1 Practice Exercise 1	
Lab 3.2 Practice Exercise 2	
Lab 3.3 Review Test 1	
Lab 3.4 Review Test 2	
Lab 3.5 Mastery Test 1	
Lab 3.6 Mastery Test 2	
Chapter 4: Implied Main Ideas and Implied Central Ideas	
Lab 4.1 Practice Exercise 1	
Lab 4.2 Practice Exercise 2	
Lab 4.3 Review Test 1	
Lab 4.4 Review Test 2	
Lab 4.5 Mastery Test 1	
Lab 4.6 Mastery Test 2	
Chapter 5: Supporting Details	
Lab 5.1 Practice Exercise 1	
Lab 5.2 Practice Exercise 2	
Lab 5.3 Review Test 1	
Lab 5.4 Review Test 2	
Lab 5.5 Mastery Test 1	
Lab 5.6 Mastery Test 2	
Chapter 6: Outlines and Concept Maps	
Lab 6.1 Practice Exercise 1	
Lab 6.2 Practice Exercise 2	
Lab 6.3 Review Test 1	
Lab 6.4 Review Test 2	
Lab 6.5 Mastery Test 1	
Lab 6.6 Mastery Test 2	

Chapter 7: Transitions and Thought Patterns	
Lab 7.1 Practice Exercise 1	
Lab 7.2 Practice Exercise 2	
Lab 7.3 Review Test 1	
Lab 7.4 Review Test 2	
Lab 7.5 Mastery Test 1	
Lab 7.6 Mastery Test 2	
Chapter 8: More Thought Patterns	
Lab 8.1 Practice Exercise 1	
Lab 8.2 Practice Exercise 2	
Lab 8.3 Review Test 1	
Lab 8.4 Review Test 2	
Lab 8.5 Mastery Test 1	
Lab 8.6 Mastery Test 2	
Chapter 9: Fact and Opinion	
Lab 9.1 Practice Exercise 1	
Lab 9.2 Practice Exercise 2	
Lab 9.3 Review Test 1	
Lab 9.4 Review Test 2	
Lab 9.5 Mastery Test 1	
Lab 9.6 Mastery Test 2	
Chapter 10: Tone and Purpose	
Lab 10.1 Practice Exercise 1	
Lab 10.2 Practice Exercise 2	
Lab 10.3 Review Test 1	
Lab 10.4 Review Test 2	
Lab 10.5 Mastery Test 1	
Lab 10.6 Mastery Test 2	
Chapter 11: Inferences	
Lab 11.1 Practice Exercise 1	
Lab 11.2 Practice Exercise 2	
Lab 11.3 Review Test 1	
Lab 11.4 Review Test 2	
Lab 11.5 Mastery Test 1	
Lab 11.6 Mastery Test 2	
Chapter 12: The Basics of Argument	
Lab 12.1 Practice Exercise 1	
Lab 12.2 Practice Exercise 2	
Lab 12.3 Review Test 1	
Lab 12.4 Review Test 2	
Lab 12.5 Mastery Test 1	
Lab 12.6 Mastery Test 2	
Chapter 13: Advanced Argument: Persuasive Techniques	
Lab 13.1 Practice Exercise 1	
Lab 13.2 Practice Exercise 2	
Lab 13.3 Review Test 1	
Lab 13.4 Review Test 2	
Lab 13.5 Mastery Test 1	
Lab 13.6 Mastery Test 2	

Practice Tests	
Practice Tests for the *Florida College Basic Skills Exit Reading Test*	
Practice Tests for the *Texas Higher Education Assessment Test*	
Practice Tests for *The Effective Reader*	
Skills Awareness Inventory: Florida Basic Exit Test	
Skills Awareness Inventory: THEA	
Skills Awareness Inventory: *The Effective Reader*	